Singapore
MATH
PRACTICE

LEVEL 5B

Appropriate for Students in GRADE 6

Frank Schaffer
An imprint of Carson-Dellosa Publishing LLC
Greensboro, North Carolina

Copyright © 2009 Singapore Asian Publications (S) Pte. Ltd.

Frank Schaffer
An imprint of Carson-Dellosa Publishing LLC
PO Box 35665
Greensboro, NC 27425 USA

Printed in the USA • All rights reserved.
3 4 5 6 GLO 13 12 11 10

ISBN 978-0-7682-4005-4
260107784

INTRODUCTION TO SINGAPORE MATH

Welcome to Singapore Math! The math curriculum in Singapore has been recognized worldwide for its excellence in producing students highly skilled in mathematics. Students in Singapore have ranked at the top in the world in mathematics on the *Trends in International Mathematics and Science Study* (TIMSS) in 1993, 1995, 2003, and 2008. Because of this, Singapore Math has gained in interest and popularity in the United States.

Singapore Math curriculum aims to help students develop the necessary math concepts and process skills for everyday life and to provide students with the ability to formulate, apply, and solve problems. Mathematics in the Singapore Primary (Elementary) Curriculum cover fewer topics but in greater depth. Key math concepts are introduced and built-on to reinforce various mathematical ideas and thinking. Students in Singapore are typically one grade level ahead of students in the United States.

The following pages provide examples of the various math problem types and skill sets taught in Singapore.

At an elementary level, some simple mathematical skills can help students understand mathematical principles. These skills are the counting-on, counting-back, and crossing-out methods. Note that these methods are most useful when the numbers are small.

1. The Counting-On Method

Used for addition of two numbers. Count on in 1s with the help of a picture or number line.

$$7 + 4 = \mathbf{11}$$

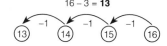

2. The Counting-Back Method

Used for subtraction of two numbers. Count back in 1s with the help of a picture or number line.

$$16 - 3 = \mathbf{13}$$

3. The Crossing-Out Method

Used for subtraction of two numbers. Cross out the number of items to be taken away. Count the remaining ones to find the answer.

$$20 - 12 = \mathbf{8}$$

A **number bond** shows the relationship in a simple addition or subtraction problem. The number bond is based on the concept "part-part-whole." This concept is useful in teaching simple addition and subtraction to young children.

To find a whole, students must add the two parts.
To find a part, students must subtract the other part from the whole.

The different types of number bonds are illustrated below.

1. Number Bond (single digits)

3 (part) + 6 (part) = **9** (whole)

9 (whole) − 3 (part) = **6** (part)

9 (whole) − 6 (part) = **3** (part)

2. Addition Number Bond (single digits)

$$= 9 + 1 + 4 \qquad \boxed{\text{Make a ten first.}}$$
$$= 10 + 4$$
$$= \mathbf{14}$$

3. Addition Number Bond (double and single digits)

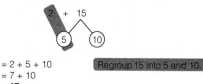

$$= 2 + 5 + 10 \qquad \boxed{\text{Regroup 15 into 5 and 10.}}$$
$$= 7 + 10$$
$$= \mathbf{17}$$

4. Subtraction Number Bond (double and single digits)

$$10 - 7 = 3$$
$$3 + 2 = \mathbf{5}$$

5. Subtraction Number Bond (double digits)

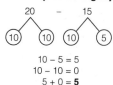

$$10 - 5 = 5$$
$$10 - 10 = 0$$
$$5 + 0 = \mathbf{5}$$

Students should understand that multiplication is repeated addition and that division is the grouping of all items into equal sets.

1. Repeated Addition (Multiplication)

Mackenzie eats 2 rolls a day. How many rolls does she eat in 5 days?

$$2 + 2 + 2 + 2 + 2 = 10$$
$$5 \times 2 = 10$$

She eats **10** rolls in 5 days.

2. The Grouping Method (Division)

Mrs. Lee makes 14 sandwiches. She gives all the sandwiches equally to 7 friends. How many sandwiches does each friend receive?

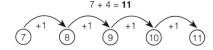

$$14 \div 7 = 2$$

Each friend receives **2** sandwiches.

One of the basic but essential math skills students should acquire is to perform the 4 operations of whole numbers and fractions. Each of these methods is illustrated below.

1. The Adding-Without-Regrouping Method

H	T	O	
3	2	1	O: Ones
+ 5	6	8	T: Tens
8	**8**	**9**	H: Hundreds

Since no regrouping is required, add the digits in each place value accordingly.

2. The Adding-by-Regrouping Method

H	T	O	
¹4	9	2	O: Ones
+ 1	5	3	T: Tens
6	**4**	**5**	H: Hundreds

In this example, regroup 14 tens into 1 hundred 4 tens.

Singapore Math Practice Level 5B

3. The Adding-by-Regrouping-Twice Method

$$
\begin{array}{cccc}
 & H & T & O \\
 & {}^{1}2 & {}^{1}8 & 6 \\
+ & 3 & 6 & 5 \\
\hline
 & 6 & 5 & 1 \\
\end{array}
$$

O: Ones
T: Tens
H: Hundreds

Regroup twice in this example.
First, regroup 11 ones into 1 ten 1 one.
Second, regroup 15 tens into 1 hundred 5 tens.

4. The Subtracting-Without-Regrouping Method

$$
\begin{array}{cccc}
 & H & T & O \\
 & 7 & 3 & 9 \\
- & 3 & 2 & 5 \\
\hline
 & 4 & 1 & 4 \\
\end{array}
$$

O: Ones
T: Tens
H: Hundreds

Since no regrouping is required, subtract the digits in each place value accordingly.

5. The Subtracting-by-Regrouping Method

$$
\begin{array}{cccc}
 & H & T & O \\
 & 5 & {}^{7}\cancel{8} & {}^{11}\cancel{1} \\
- & 2 & 4 & 7 \\
\hline
 & 3 & 3 & 4 \\
\end{array}
$$

O: Ones
T: Tens
H: Hundreds

In this example, students cannot subtract 7 ones from 1 one. So, regroup the tens and ones. Regroup 8 tens 1 one into 7 tens 11 ones.

6. The Subtracting-by-Regrouping-Twice Method

$$
\begin{array}{cccc}
 & H & T & O \\
 & {}^{7}\cancel{8} & {}^{9}\cancel{0} & {}^{10}\cancel{0} \\
- & 5 & 9 & 3 \\
\hline
 & 2 & 0 & 7 \\
\end{array}
$$

O: Ones
T: Tens
H: Hundreds

In this example, students cannot subtract 3 ones from 0 ones and 9 tens from 0 tens. So, regroup the hundreds, tens, and ones. Regroup 8 hundreds into 7 hundreds 9 tens 10 ones.

7. The Multiplying-Without-Regrouping Method

$$
\begin{array}{ccc}
 & T & O \\
 & 2 & 4 \\
\times & & 2 \\
\hline
 & 4 & 8 \\
\end{array}
$$

O: Ones
T: Tens

Since no regrouping is required, multiply the digit in each place value by the multiplier accordingly.

8. The Multiplying-With-Regrouping Method

$$
\begin{array}{cccc}
 & H & T & O \\
 & {}^{1}3 & {}^{2}4 & 9 \\
\times & & & 3 \\
\hline
1, & 0 & 4 & 7 \\
\end{array}
$$

O: Ones
T: Tens
H: Hundreds

In this example, regroup 27 ones into 2 tens 7 ones, and 14 tens into 1 hundred 4 tens.

9. The Dividing-Without-Regrouping Method

$$
\begin{array}{r}
2\,4\,1 \\
2\overline{)4\,8\,2} \\
\underline{-4} \\
8 \\
\underline{-8} \\
2 \\
\underline{-2} \\
0 \\
\end{array}
$$

Since no regrouping is required, divide the digit in each place value by the divisor accordingly.

10. The Dividing-With-Regrouping Method

$$
\begin{array}{r}
1\,6\,6 \\
5\overline{)8\,3\,0} \\
\underline{-5} \\
3\,3 \\
\underline{-3\,0} \\
3\,0 \\
\underline{-3\,0} \\
0 \\
\end{array}
$$

In this example, regroup 3 hundreds into 30 tens and add 3 tens to make 33 tens. Regroup 3 tens into 30 ones.

11. The Addition-of-Fractions Method

$$
\frac{1}{6} \times \frac{2}{2} + \frac{1}{4} \times \frac{3}{3} = \frac{2}{12} + \frac{3}{12} = \frac{5}{12}
$$

Always remember to make the denominators common before adding the fractions.

12. The Subtraction-of-Fractions Method

$$
\frac{1}{2} \times \frac{5}{5} - \frac{1}{5} \times \frac{2}{2} = \frac{5}{10} - \frac{2}{10} = \frac{3}{10}
$$

Always remembers to make the denominators common before subtracting the fractions.

13. The Multiplication-of-Fractions Method

$$
\frac{{}^{1}\cancel{3}}{5} \times \frac{1}{{}_{3}\cancel{9}} = \frac{1}{15}
$$

When the numerator and the denominator have a common multiple, reduce them to their lowest fractions.

14. The Division-of-Fractions Method

$$
\frac{7}{9} \div \frac{1}{6} = \frac{7}{{}_{3}\cancel{9}} \times \frac{\cancel{6}^{2}}{1} = \frac{14}{3} = 4\frac{2}{3}
$$

When dividing fractions, first change the division sign ($\div$) to the multiplication sign ($\times$). Then, switch the numerator and denominator of the fraction on the right hand side. Multiply the fractions in the usual way.

Model drawing is an effective strategy used to solve math word problems. It is a visual representation of the information in word problems using bar units. By drawing the models, students will know of the variables given in the problem, the variables to find, and even the methods used to solve the problem.

Drawing models is also a versatile strategy. It can be applied to simple word problems involving addition, subtraction, multiplication, and division. It can also be applied to word problems related to fractions, decimals, percentage, and ratio.

The use of models also trains students to think in an algebraic manner, which uses symbols for representation.

The different types of bar models used to solve word problems are illustrated below.

1. The model that involves addition

Melissa has 50 blue beads and 20 red beads. How many beads does she have altogether?

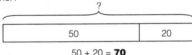

$50 + 20 = \textbf{70}$

2. The model that involves subtraction

Ben and Andy have 90 toy cars. Andy has 60 toy cars. How many toy cars does Ben have?

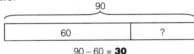

$90 - 60 = \textbf{30}$

3. The model that involves comparison

Mr. Simons has 150 magazines and 110 books in his study. How many more magazines than books does he have?

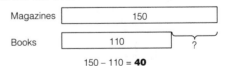

$150 - 110 = \textbf{40}$

4. The model that involves two items with a difference

A pair of shoes costs $109. A leather bag costs $241 more than the pair of shoes. How much is the leather bag?

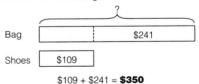

$\$109 + \$241 = \textbf{\$350}$

Singapore Math Practice Level 5B

5. The model that involves multiples

Mrs. Drew buys 12 apples. She buys 3 times as many oranges as apples. She also buys 3 times as many cherries as oranges. How many pieces of fruit does she buy altogether?

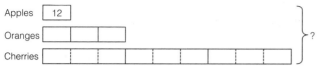

$$13 \times 12 = \textbf{156}$$

6. The model that involves multiples and difference

There are 15 students in Class A. There are 5 more students in Class B than in Class A. There are 3 times as many students in Class C than in Class A. How many students are there altogether in the three classes?

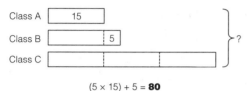

$$(5 \times 15) + 5 = \textbf{80}$$

7. The model that involves creating a whole

Ellen, Giselle, and Brenda bake 111 muffins. Giselle bakes twice as many muffins as Brenda. Ellen bakes 9 fewer muffins than Giselle. How many muffins does Ellen bake?

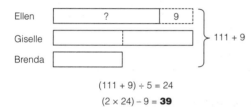

$$(111 + 9) \div 5 = 24$$
$$(2 \times 24) - 9 = \textbf{39}$$

8. The model that involves sharing

There are 183 tennis balls in Basket A and 97 tennis balls in Basket B. How many tennis balls must be transferred from Basket A to Basket B so that both baskets contain the same number of tennis balls?

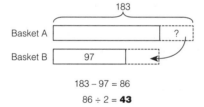

$$183 - 97 = 86$$
$$86 \div 2 = \textbf{43}$$

9. The model that involves fractions

George had 355 marbles. He lost $\frac{1}{5}$ of the marbles and gave $\frac{1}{4}$ of the remaining marbles to his brother. How many marbles did he have left?

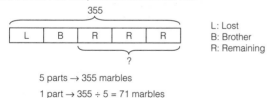

L: Lost
B: Brother
R: Remaining

5 parts → 355 marbles
1 part → 355 ÷ 5 = 71 marbles
3 parts → 3 × 71 = **213** marbles

10. The model that involves ratio

Aaron buys a tie and a belt. The prices of the tie and belt are in the ratio 2 : 5. If both items cost $539,

(a) what is the price of the tie?

(b) what is the price of the belt?

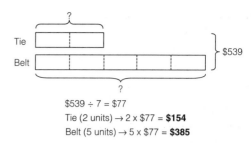

$$\$539 \div 7 = \$77$$
Tie (2 units) → 2 x $77 = **$154**
Belt (5 units) → 5 x $77 = **$385**

11. The model that involves comparison of fractions

Jack's height is $\frac{2}{3}$ of Leslie's height. Leslie's height is $\frac{3}{4}$ of Lindsay's height. If Lindsay is 160 cm tall, find Jack's height and Leslie's height.

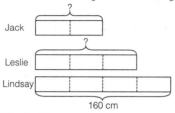

1 unit → 160 ÷ 4 = 40 cm

Leslie's height (3 units) → 3 × 40 = **120 cm**

Jack's height (2 units) → 2 × 40 = **80 cm**

Thinking skills and strategies are important in mathematical problem solving. These skills are applied when students think through the math problems to solve them. Below are some commonly used thinking skills and strategies applied in mathematical problem solving.

1. Comparing

Comparing is a form of thinking skill that students can apply to identify similarities and differences.

When comparing numbers, look carefully at each digit before deciding if a number is greater or less than the other. Students might also use a number line for comparison when there are more numbers.

Example:

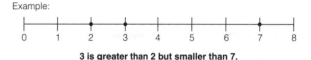

3 is greater than 2 but smaller than 7.

2. Sequencing

A sequence shows the order of a series of numbers. *Sequencing* is a form of thinking skill that requires students to place numbers in a particular order. There are many terms in a sequence. The terms refer to the numbers in a sequence.

To place numbers in a correct order, students must first find a rule that generates the sequence. In a simple math sequence, students can either add or subtract to find the unknown terms in the sequence.

Example: Find the 7th term in the sequence below.

1,	4,	7,	10,	13,	16	?
1st term	2nd term	3rd term	4th term	5th term	6th term	7th term

Step 1: This sequence is in an increasing order.

Step 2: 4 − 1 = 3   7 − 4 = 3
The difference between two consecutive terms is 3.

Step 3: 16 + 3 = 19
The 7th term is **19**.

3. Visualization

Visualization is a problem solving strategy that can help students visualize a problem through the use of physical objects. Students will play a more active role in solving the problem by manipulating these objects.

The main advantage of using this strategy is the mobility of information in the process of solving the problem. When students make a wrong step in the process, they can retrace the step without erasing or canceling it.

The other advantage is that this strategy helps develop a better understanding of the problem or solution through visual objects or images. In this way, students will be better able to remember how to solve these types of problems.

Some of the commonly used objects for this strategy are toothpicks, straws, cards, strings, water, sand, pencils, paper, and dice.

4. Look for a Pattern

This strategy requires the use of observational and analytical skills. Students have to observe the given data to find a pattern in order to solve the problem. Math word problems that involve the use of this strategy usually have repeated numbers or patterns.

Example: Find the sum of all the numbers from 1 to 100.

Step 1: Simplify the problem.

Find the sum of 1, 2, 3, 4, 5, 6, 7, 8, 9, and 10.

Step 2: Look for a pattern.

$1 + 10 = 11$	$2 + 9 = 11$	$3 + 8 = 11$
$4 + 7 = 11$	$5 + 6 = 11$	

Step 3: Describe the pattern.

When finding the sum of 1 to 10, add the first and last numbers to get a result of 11. Then, add the second and second last numbers to get the same result. The pattern continues until all the numbers from 1 to 10 are added. There will be 5 pairs of such results. Since each addition equals 11, the answer is then $5 \times 11 = 55$.

Step 4: Use the pattern to find the answer.

Since there are 5 pairs in the sum of 1 to 10, there should be ($10 \times 5 = 50$ pairs) in the sum of 1 to 100.

Note that the addition for each pair is not equal to 11 now. The addition for each pair is now ($1 + 100 = 101$).

$$50 \times 101 = 5050$$

The sum of all the numbers from 1 to 100 is **5,050**.

5. Working Backward

The strategy of working backward applies only to a specific type of math word problem. These word problems state the end result, and students are required to find the total number. In order to solve these word problems, students have to work backward by thinking through the correct sequence of events. The strategy of working backward allows students to use their logical reasoning and sequencing to find the answers.

Example: Sarah has a piece of ribbon. She cuts the ribbon into 4 equal parts. Each part is then cut into 3 smaller equal parts. If the length of each small part is 35 cm, how long is the piece of ribbon?

$$3 \times 35 = 105 \text{ cm}$$
$$4 \times 105 = 420 \text{ cm}$$

The piece of ribbon is **420 cm**.

6. The Before-After Concept

The *Before-After* concept lists all the relevant data before and after an event. Students can then compare the differences and eventually solve the problems. Usually, the Before-After concept and the mathematical model go hand in hand to solve math word problems. Note that the Before-After concept can be applied only to a certain type of math word problem, which trains students to think sequentially.

Example: Kelly has 4 times as much money as Joey. After Kelly uses some money to buy a tennis racquet, and Joey uses $30 to buy a pair of pants, Kelly has twice as much money as Joey. If Joey has $98 in the beginning,
(a) how much money does Kelly have in the end?
(b) how much money does Kelly spend on the tennis racquet?

Before

Kelly | | | | |
Joey | $98 |

After

Kelly
Joey | | $30 |

(a) $98 - $30 = $68
$2 \times $68 = 136
Kelly has **$136** in the end.

(b) $4 \times $98 = 392
$392 − $136 = 256
Kelly spends **$256** on the tennis racquet.

7. Making Supposition

Making supposition is commonly known as "making an assumption." Students can use this strategy to solve certain types of math word problems. Making assumptions will eliminate some possibilities and simplifies the word problems by providing a boundary of values to work within.

Example: Mrs. Jackson bought 100 pieces of candy for all the students in her class. How many pieces of candy would each student receive if there were 25 students in her class?

In the above word problem, assume that each student received the same number of pieces. This eliminates the possibilities that some students would receive more than others due to good behaviour, better results, or any other reason.

8. Representation of Problem

In problem solving, students often use representations in the solutions to show their understanding of the problems. Using representations also allow students to understand the mathematical concepts and relationships as well as to manipulate the information presented in the problems. Examples of representations are diagrams and lists or tables.

Diagrams allow students to consolidate or organize the information given in the problems. By drawing a diagram, students can see the problem clearly and solve it effectively.

A list or table can help students organize information that is useful for analysis. After analyzing, students can then see a pattern, which can be used to solve the problem.

9. Guess and Check

One of the most important and effective problem-solving techniques is *Guess and Check*. It is also known as *Trial and Error*. As the name suggests, students have to guess the answer to a problem and check if that guess is correct. If the guess is wrong, students will make another guess. This will continue until the guess is correct.

It is beneficial to keep a record of all the guesses and checks in a table. In addition, a *Comments* column can be included. This will enable students to analyze their guess (if it is too high or too low) and improve on the next guess. Be careful; this problem-solving technique can be tiresome without systematic or logical guesses.

Example: Jessica had 15 coins. Some of them were 10-cent coins and the rest were 5-cent coins. The total amount added up to $1.25. How many coins of each kind were there?

Use the guess-and-check method.

Number of 10¢ Coins	Value	Number of 5¢ Coins	Value	Total Number of Coins	Total Value
7	$7 \times 10¢ = 70¢$	8	$8 \times 5¢ = 40¢$	$7 + 8 = 15$	$70¢ + 40¢ = 110¢ = \$1.10$
8	$8 \times 10¢ = 80¢$	7	$7 \times 5¢ = 35¢$	$8 + 7 = 15$	$80¢ + 35¢ = 115¢ = \$1.15$
10	$10 \times 10¢ = 100¢$	5	$5 \times 5¢ = 25¢$	$10 + 5 = 15$	$100¢ + 25¢ = 125¢ = \$1.25$

There were **ten** 10-cent coins and **five** 5-cent coins.

10. Restate the Problem

When solving challenging math problems, conventional methods may not be workable. Instead, restating the problem will enable students to see some challenging problems in a different light so that they can better understand them.

The strategy of restating the problem is to "say" the problem in a different and clearer way. However, students have to ensure that the main idea of the problem is not altered.

How do students restate a math problem?

First, read and understand the problem. Gather the given facts and unknowns. Note any condition(s) that have to be satisfied.

Next, restate the problem. Imagine narrating this problem to a friend. Present the given facts, unknown(s), and condition(s). Students may want to write the "revised" problem. Once the "revised" problem is analyzed, students should be able to think of an appropriate strategy to solve it.

11. Simplify the Problem

One of the commonly used strategies in mathematical problem solving is simplification of the problem. When a problem is simplified, it can be "broken down" into two or more smaller parts. Students can then solve the parts systematically to get to the final answer.

Singapore Math Practice Level 5B

Table of Contents

Singapore Math Practice Level 5B

LEARNING OUTCOMES

Unit 7 More on Decimals

Students should be able to

- convert decimals to fractions.
- multiply and divide decimals by tens, hundreds, and thousands without the use of calculators.
- perform 4 operations of decimals using calculators.
- solve story problems related to decimals.

Unit 8 Conversion of Metric Measurements

Students should be able to

- convert meters to centimeters, kilometers to meters, kilograms to grams, and liters to milliliters.
- convert centimeters to meters, meters to kilometers, grams to kilograms, and milliliters to liters.
- solve related story problems.

Review 1

This review tests students' understanding of Units 7 & 8.

Unit 9 Averages

Students should be able to

- understand the concept of averages.
- calculate averages.
- calculate a total number based on an average and the number of items given.
- solve story problems related to averages.

Unit 10 Percentages

Students should be able to

- convert percentages to decimals or fractions.
- convert decimals or fractions to percentages.
- convert part of a quantity into a percentage.
- calculate quantity based on a percentage.
- solve story problems related to percentages.

Review 2

This review tests students' understanding of Units 9 & 10.

Unit 11 Angles

Students should be able to

- recognize angles on a straight line, angles at a point, and vertically opposite angles.
- use the above-mentioned properties to find unknown angles.

Unit 12 Triangles and 4-Sided Figures

Students should be able to

- recognize and find unknown angles in right-angled, isosceles, and equilateral triangles.
- recognize and find unknown angles in a parallelogram, rhombus, and trapezoid.

Review 3

This review tests students' understanding of Units 11 & 12.

Unit 13 Geometrical Construction

Students should be able to

- construct triangles, squares, rectangles, parallelograms, rhombuses, and trapezoids.

Unit 14 Volume

Students should be able to

- calculate the number of unit cubes in a solid.
- draw a cube or cuboid on a dot grid.
- find the volume of a solid using a formula.
- convert volume between cm^3, L, and mL.
- find the volume of liquid in a container.
- solve story problems related to volume.

Review 4

This review tests students' understanding of Units 13 & 14.

Final Review

This review serves as a practice test and is an excellent assessment of students' understanding of all the topics in this book.

FORMULA SHEET

Unit 7   More on Decimals

To multiply decimals by
10, move the decimal point 1 place to the right.
100, move the decimal point 2 places to the right.
1,000, move the decimal point 3 places to the right.

To divide decimals by
10, move the decimal point 1 place to the left.
100, move the decimal point 2 places to the left.
1,000, move the decimal point 3 places to the left.

Unit 8   Conversion of Metric Measurements

meters to centimeters= × 100
kilometers to meters= × 1,000
kilograms to grams= × 1,000

centimeters to meters= ÷ 100
meters to kilometers= ÷ 1,000
grams to kilograms= ÷ 1,000
milliliters to liters= ÷ 1,000

Unit 9   Averages

average = total number ÷ number of items
total number = average × number of items

Unit 10 Percentages

fraction to percentage= fraction × 100
decimal to percentage= decimal × 100

$$\text{percentage to fraction}= \frac{\text{number in percentage}}{100}$$

(Remember to write in the simplest form.)

percentage to decimal= percentage ÷ 100
To find the percentage of a quantity, multiply percentage by total quantity.

To find a discount, multiply the discount percentage by the usual price of the item.
To find the final price, subtract the discount from the usual price of the item.

To find interest, multiply the interest rate by the principal amount.
To find the final amount, add the interest to the principal amount.

Unit 11 Angles

Properties of angles
- The sum of angles on a straight line is 180°.
- The sum of angles at a point is 360°.
- Vertically opposite angles are equal.

Unit 12 Triangles and 4-Sided Figures

Property of a triangle
- The sum of all angles in a triangle is 180°.

Properties of a right-angled triangle
- One angle is 90°.
- The sum of the other 2 angles is 90°.

Properties of an isosceles triangle
- It has 2 equal sides.
- It has 2 equal angles.

Properties of an equilateral triangle
- It has 3 equal sides.
- It has 3 equal angles.

Properties of a parallelogram
- Opposite sides are equal and parallel.
- Opposite angles are equal.
- The pair of angles between 2 parallel sides adds up to 180°.

Properties of a rhombus
- It has 4 equal sides.
- Opposite sides are parallel.
- Opposite angles are equal.
- The pair of angles between 2 parallel sides adds up to 180°.

Properties of a trapezoid
- It has one pair of opposite parallel sides.
- The pair of angles between the parallel sides adds up to 180°.

Unit 14 Volume

1 L = 1,000 mL = 1,000 cm^3
Volume of cube = Edge × Edge × Edge
Volume of cuboid = Length × Width × Height

Unit 7: MORE ON DECIMALS

Examples:

1. $3.56 \times 10 = \underline{\textbf{35.6}}$

2. $1.05 \times 500 = 1.05 \times 5 \times 100$

   $\qquad\qquad = 5.25 \times 100$

   $\qquad\qquad = \underline{\textbf{525}}$

3. $0.49 \times 8{,}000 = 0.49 \times 8 \times 1{,}000$

   $\qquad\qquad\quad = \underline{\textbf{3,920}}$

4. $45 \div 50 = 45 \div 5 \div 10$

   $\qquad\quad = 9 \div 10$

   $\qquad\quad = \underline{\textbf{0.9}}$

5. $61.5 \div 300 = 61.5 \div 3 \div 100$

   $\qquad\qquad = 20.5 \div 100$

   $\qquad\qquad = \underline{\textbf{0.205}}$

6. $2{,}831 \div 1{,}000 = \underline{\textbf{2.831}}$

Singapore Math Practice Level 5B

Convert the following decimals to fractions or mixed numbers. Write each in its simplest form.

1. $0.5 =$ _____

2. $6.9 =$ _____

3. $46.6 =$ _____

4. $258.3 =$ _____

5. $0.02 =$ _____

6. $7.36 =$ _____

7. $69.15 =$ _____

8. $420.07 =$ _____

9. $0.003 =$ _____

10. $8.802 =$ _____

11. $59.575 =$ _____

12. $952.007 =$ _____

Multiply the following decimals. Write the correct answers on the lines.

13. $0.5 \times 10 =$ _____

14. $44.9 \times 10 =$ _____

15. $105.67 \times 10 =$ _____

16. $26.093 \times 10 =$ _____

17. $0.08 \times 100 =$ _____

18. $37.71 \times 100 =$ _____

19. $480.409 \times 100 =$ _____

20. $0.28 \times 1,000 =$ _____

21. $184.6 \times 1,000 =$ _____

22. $475.36 \times 1,000 =$ _____

23. $0.32 \times$ _____ $= 3.2$

24. $0.7 \times$ _____ $= 70$

25. $90.01 \times$ _____ $= 9,001$

26. _____ $\times 10 = 1.48$

27. _____ $\times 100 = 6.5$

28. _____ $\times 1,000 = 500$

Singapore Math Practice Level 5B

29. $0.2 \times 40 = 0.2 \times$ _____ $\times$ _____ $=$ _____

30. $68.35 \times 90 = 68.35 \times$ _____ $\times$ _____ $=$ _____

31. $9.4 \times 300 = 9.4 \times$ _____ $\times$ _____ $=$ _____

32. $204.56 \times 700 = 204.56 \times$ _____ $\times$ _____ $=$ _____

33. $50.9 \times 6,000 = 50.9 \times$ _____ $\times$ _____ $=$ _____

34. $74.21 \times 3,000 = 74.21 \times$ _____ $\times$ _____ $=$ _____

35. $1,215 =$ _____ $\times 10 =$ _____ $\times 100 =$ _____ $\times 1,000$

36. $4,849 = 484.9 \times$ _____ $= 48.49 \times$ _____ $= 4.849 \times$ _____

37. $12,008 =$ _____ $\times 10 =$ _____ $\times 100 =$ _____ $\times 1,000$

Divide the following decimals. Write the correct answers on the lines.

38. $7 \div 10 =$ _____

39. $0.9 \div 10 =$ _____

40. $95.73 \div 10 =$ _____

41. $78.7 \div 100 =$ _____

42. $5,461 \div 100 =$ _____

43. $1,003 \div 1,000 =$ _____

44. $20,120 \div 1,000 =$ _____

45. $71.62 \div$ _____ $= 7.162$

46. $187.9 \div$ _____ $= 1.879$

47. $807 \div$ _____ $= 0.807$

48. _____ $\div 10 = 0.218$

49. _____ $\div 100 = 3.649$

50. _____ $\div 1,000 = 0.092$

51. _____ $\div 1,000 = 13.55$

13

52. $2.4 \div 20 = 2.4 \div \underline{\hspace{1.5cm}} \div \underline{\hspace{1.5cm}} = \underline{\hspace{2cm}}$

53. $4.05 \div 50 = 4.05 \div \underline{\hspace{1.5cm}} \div \underline{\hspace{1.5cm}} = \underline{\hspace{2cm}}$

54. $84 \div 700 = 84 \div \underline{\hspace{1.5cm}} \div \underline{\hspace{1.5cm}} = \underline{\hspace{2cm}}$

55. $178 \div 400 = 178 \div \underline{\hspace{1.5cm}} \div \underline{\hspace{1.5cm}} = \underline{\hspace{2cm}}$

56. $90 \div 3,000 = 90 \div \underline{\hspace{1.5cm}} \div \underline{\hspace{1.5cm}} = \underline{\hspace{2cm}}$

57. $954 \div 6,000 = 954 \div \underline{\hspace{1.5cm}} \div \underline{\hspace{1.5cm}} = \underline{\hspace{2cm}}$

58. $6.27 = \underline{\hspace{1.5cm}} \div 10 = \underline{\hspace{1.5cm}} \div 100 = \underline{\hspace{1.5cm}} \div 1,000$

59. $179.4 = \underline{\hspace{1.5cm}} \div 10 = \underline{\hspace{1.5cm}} \div 100 = \underline{\hspace{1.5cm}} \div 1,000$

60. $24.8 = 24,800 \div \underline{\hspace{1.5cm}} = 2,480 \div \underline{\hspace{1.5cm}} = 248 \div \underline{\hspace{1.5cm}}$

Solve the following problems using a calculator.

61. $\$23.55 + \$17.95 = \underline{\hspace{2cm}}$

62. $100.3 \text{ cm} - 62.08 \text{ cm} = \underline{\hspace{2cm}}$

63. $45.7 \text{ yd.} \times 90 = \underline{\hspace{2cm}}$

64. $53.915 \text{ kg} \div 5 = \underline{\hspace{2cm}}$

65. $\$25.35 \times 19 = \underline{\hspace{2cm}}$

66. Add 107.83 gal. and 64.18 gal. = $\underline{\hspace{2cm}}$

14

67. Subtract $937.95 from $3,549.20 = _____

68. Multiply 2.864 gal. by 47 = _____

69. Divide 736.4 lb. by 35 = _____

70. Subtract 20.346 L from 548.6 L = _____

Solve the following story problems. Show your work in the space below. You may use a calculator whenever you see [calculator icon].

71. A dozen T-shirts cost $162.60. How much does each T-shirt cost?

72. Mrs. Matthews bought 12.45 kg of shrimp and $\frac{3}{4}$ kg of salmon. If the shrimp cost $30 per kg and the salmon cost $18 per kg, how much did Mrs. Matthews spend altogether?

73. The mass of a metal container, together with 10 identical metal balls, is 79.15 lb. If the mass of the metal container is 16.75 lb., what is the mass of each metal ball?

74. Joey bought 17.3 m of cloth. $\frac{1}{5}$ of the cloth was damaged and he used the rest to make 4 curtains.

   (a)   How much cloth did Joey use to make 1 curtain?

   (b)   If Joey sold each curtain for $19.90, how much money would he make altogether?

75. Katrina divided 8.6 lb. of sugar into 5 equal portions. She kept 2 portions for herself and gave the rest to her sister. Her sister used 1.15 lb. of sugar to bake some cakes. How much sugar did her sister have left?

Singapore Math Practice Level 5B

76. A box of pencils costs $3.25 and a box of colored pencils costs $4.65. However, a box of pencils and a box of colored pencils are sold together at $6.50. If Alex wants to buy 6 boxes of pencils and 9 boxes of colored pencils, what is the least amount of money that Alex can pay?

Unit 8: CONVERSION OF METRIC MEASUREMENTS

Examples:

1. Convert 200.9 kg to grams (g).

   200.9 × 1,000 = **200,900 g**

2. Convert 462.5 cm to meters (m).

   462.5 ÷ 100 = **4.625 m**

Find the equivalent measurements. Write the correct answers on the lines.

1. Convert 7.05 m to centimeters (cm).   _____

2. Convert 9.163 m to centimeters (cm).   _____

3. Convert 100.2 m to centimeters (cm).   _____

4. Convert 1.755 km to meters (m).   _____

5. Convert 24.82 km to meters (m).   _____

6. Convert 69.95 km to meters (m).   _____

7. Convert 5.105 kg to grams (g).   _____

8. Convert 30.4 kg to grams (g).   _____

9. Convert 171.7 kg to grams (g).   _____

10. Convert 0.126 L to milliliters (mL).   _____

11. Convert 8.103 L to milliliters (mL).   _____

12. Convert 19.6 L to milliliters (mL).   _____

Singapore Math Practice Level 5B

13. Write 70.095 kg in kilograms and grams. _____

14. Write 66.04 L in liters and milliliters. _____

15. Write 13.96 m in meters and centimeters. _____

16. Write 45.5 m in meters and centimeters. _____

17. Write 4.137 L in liters and milliliters. _____

18. Write 8.016 m in kilometers and meters. _____

19. Write 312.4 m in meters and centimeters. _____

20. Write 4.58 kg in kilograms and grams. _____

Find the equivalent measurements. Write the correct answers on the lines.

21. Convert 439 cm to meters (m). _____

22. Convert 88.3 cm to meters (m). _____

23. Convert 969.5 cm to meters (m). _____

24. Convert 18 m to kilometers (km). _____

25. Convert 616 m to kilometers (km). _____

26. Convert 3,504 m to kilometers (km). _____

27. Convert 97 g to kilograms (kg). _____

28. Convert 402 g to kilograms (kg). _____

29. Convert 3,610 g to kilograms (kg). _____

30. Convert 25 mL to liters (L). _____

31. Convert 708 mL to liters (L). _____

32. Convert 60,900 mL to liters (L).   _____

33. Write 52 m 40 cm as a decimal in meters.   _____

34. Write 9 km 25 m as a decimal in kilometers.   _____

35. Write 8 kg 9 g as a decimal in kilograms.   _____

36. Write 98 L 200 mL as a decimal in liters.   _____

37. Write 37 kg 35 g as a decimal in kilograms.   _____

38. Write 528 L 5 mL as a decimal in liters.   _____

39. Write 127 m 33 cm as a decimal in meters.   _____

40. Write 580 km 600 m as a decimal in kilometers.   _____

Solve the following story problems. Show your work in the space below. You may use a calculator whenever you see ▨.

41. The mass of a bag of rice is 5 kg. What is the total mass in grams of 15 bags of rice?

Singapore Math Practice Level 5B

42. A custodian uses 36 buckets of water to clean 9 bathroom. The bucket has a capacity of 5.5 liters. If she fills the bucket of water to the brim each time, find the amount of water she uses to wash each bathroom in milliliters. Assume she uses the same number of buckets of water to clean each bathroom.

43. A bus driver drives 21.95 km from one bus stop to another. If the bus driver makes 3 round trips each day, find the total distance in meters he drives per day.

44. A store owner buys 6 cartons of canned drinks. There are 24 cans of drinks in each carton. Each can contains 390 mL of liquid. He empties all the cans into a big container for a charity show. How many liters of drinks are in the big container?

45. Erika uses 195 cm of ribbon to make 13 identical bookmarks. Find the length of ribbon in meters that she uses to make 175 bookmarks.

Singapore Math Practice Level 5B

46. A chef uses 175 g of flour to make a pizza.

    (a)   If he makes 255 pizzas within 5 days, how many pizzas does the chef make per year? Assume the chef makes pizzas every day of the year.

    (b)   How many kilograms of flour does the chef need per year?

REVIEW 1

Choose the correct answer, and write its number in the parentheses. You may use a calculator whenever you see 📠.

1. Express 10.037 km in kilometers and meters.

   (1) 10 km 37 m   (3) 100 km 37 m
   (2) 10 km 370 m   (4) 100 km 370 m   (   )

2. $8 \div 1,000 =$ _____

   (1) 0.008   (3) 0.8
   (2) 0.08   (4) 8,000   (   )

3. Convert 18.25 to a fraction in its simplest form.

   (1) $18\frac{1}{2}$ (3) $18\frac{1}{3}$
   (2) $18\frac{2}{5}$ (4) $18\frac{1}{4}$ (   )

4. Convert 49.7 cm to meters (m).

   (1) 0.0497 m   (3) 4.97 m
   (2) 0.497 m   (4) 4,970 m   (   )

5. A bag of sugar has a mass of 800 g. Find the total mass of 25 bags of sugar in kilograms.

   (1) 2 kg   (3) 200 kg
   (2) 20 kg   (4) 20,000 kg   (   )

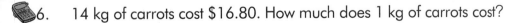

6. 14 kg of carrots cost $16.80. How much does 1 kg of carrots cost?

   (1) $1.20   (3) $23.52
   (2) $12   (4) $235.20   (   )

Singapore Math Practice Level 5B

7. A sum of $585 is shared equally among Kelly and her 5 sisters. Kelly uses all her money to purchase 10 notebooks. How much does each notebook cost?

    (1) $9.75   (3) $97.50
    (2) $11.70   (4) $117   (   )

Write your answers on the lines. You may use a calculator whenever you see 🖩.

8. Write 470 L 500 mL as a decimal in liters.   _____

9. Subtract $209.95 from $7,885.60.   _____

10. Convert 13.405 kg to grams (g).   _____

11. Find 7.08 × 500.   _____

12. June uses 22 identical sticks to make a rectangular frame. The width of the frame requires 4 sticks. Each stick is 7.5 cm long. What is the height of the frame in meters?

                                                                     _____

13. ☐ × 10 × 100 × 1,000 = 197,000.

    What is the correct answer in the box?

                                                                     _____

14. To get an answer of 8.4, Nicholas has to multiply Number A by 7 and then multiply it by 10. What is Number A?

                                                                     _____

15. To enroll in a 30-hour Spanish class, students must pay $481.50. If the language center collected a total of $19,260, how many people enrolled in the Spanish class?

                                                                     _____

Singapore Math Practice Level 5B

Solve the following story problems. Show your work in the space below. You may use a calculator whenever you see .

16. Noah bought a carton of 24 bottles of mineral water. Each bottle of water was 330 mL. Find the total capacity of the carton of mineral water. Write your answer in liters.

17. Mr. Ali ordered 1,000 prepared lunches for a company trip. He ordered another 80 vegetarian lunches for the same trip. Each lunch cost $3.30 and each vegetarian lunch cost $4.20. How much did Mr. Ali pay for all the lunches?

18. A supermarket wants to equally package 500 kg of frozen chicken wings. Each package of frozen chicken wings will have a mass of 20 kg.

(a) How many packages of frozen chicken wings are there?

(b) If Mrs. Daves buys 3 packages of frozen chicken wings and each package costs $15.55, how much will she pay?

19. Chloe buys a dozen cartons of milk, each containing 0.85 liters of milk. If her family drink 0.75 liters of milk every day, how many milliliters of milk are left after a week?

20. The distance to run one lap on a school track is 0.4 km. Zachary runs 8 laps and Cheng runs 5 laps.

    (a) Find the total distance in meters both boys have run.

    (b) How much farther has Zachary run than Cheng?

Singapore Math Practice Level 5B

Unit 9: AVERAGES

Example:

Find the average of 18, 36, and 54.

$$\text{Total} = 18 + 36 + 54$$
$$= 108$$

$$\text{Average} = 108 \div 3$$
$$= 36$$

The average of 18, 36, and 54 is **36**.

Write the correct answers on the lines.

1. (a) Find the total of $15, $18, and $60. _____

   (b) Find the average. _____

2. (a) Find the total of 268 kg, 208 kg, and 109 kg. _____

   (b) Find the average. _____

3. (a) Find the total of 35 in., 81 in., 66 in., and 94 in. _____

   (b) Find the average. _____

Singapore Math Practice Level 5B

4. (a) Find the total of 358 L, 92 L, 189 L, and 93 L.   _____

    (b) Find the average.   _____

5. (a) Find the total of 293 in., 158 in., 431 in., and 126 in. _____

    (b) Find the average.   _____

Calculate the average of each set of numbers. You may use a calculator whenever you see 🖩.

6. 6, 9, and 15   _____

7. 1, 11, and 21   _____

8. 14, 56, 73, and 105   _____

9. 10, 20, 30, 40, and 50   _____

10. 9, 18, 36, 72, and 126   _____

🖩11. $3.50, $6.05, and $11   _____

🖩12. 0.75 kg, 1.4 kg, 3.36 kg, 9.6 kg, and 21.09 kg   _____

13. 15.5 gal., 8.7 gal., 5.3 gal., and 3.9 gal.   _____

14. 48.7 km, 99.3 km, and 132.5 km   _____

🖩15. 46 min., 52 min., 84 min., 93 min., and 106 min.   _____

Singapore Math Practice Level 5B

Solve the following story problems. Show your work in the space below. You may use a calculator whenever you see [calculator].

16. The table below shows the amount of money Karim saved during 5 consecutive months.

April	May	June	July	August
$200	$180	$280	$300	$265

What was the average amount of money Karim saved during this period of time?

17. The table below shows the height of 4 boys.

Adam	Connor	Daniel	Javier
145 cm	152 cm	?	150 cm

If the average height of the 4 boys is 146.5 cm, find Daniel's height.

18. The table below shows the points Rose scored on a test.

Subjects	English	Mathematics	Science	Social Studies
Points	72	85	70	79

(a) Find the total points for the 4 subjects.

(b) Find the average points for the 4 subjects.

19. The table below shows different types of vehicles that passed by a shop in a day.

Types of vehicles	Cars	Vans	Motorcycles	Buses	Bicycles
Number of vehicles	608	411	?	227	?

The average number of vehicles that passed by the shop on that day was 369. The number of motorcycles was 569 more than the number of bicycles. Find the number of bicycles that passed by the shop on that day.

Singapore Math Practice Level 5B

20. The average of 4 numbers is 24.5. If 3 of the numbers are 16, 47, and 25, what is the last number?

21. A shopkeeper sold an average of 329 cans of drinks per day for a week at a fair. If he had sold an average of 250 cans of drinks for the first 5 days, how many cans of drinks did he sell during the last 2 days?

22. A box filled with pens has a mass of 12.8 kg. The box has a mass of 800 g when it is empty. If the average mass of all the pens is 160 g, how many pens are there in the box?

23. There are 22 girls and 18 boys in a class. If the total lunch money of all the boys is $27 and the average lunch money of all the girls is $0.90, find the average lunch money of all the students in the class.

24. Find the average of all the whole numbers ranging from 1 to 20.

25. There are some green and red apples in a box. The total mass of all the green apples is 5,250 g. The total mass of all the apples is 8,450 g. Find the number of red apples in the box if the average mass of all the red apples is 200 g.

26. Uncle Ron had 10 boxes of red pens and 15 boxes of blue pens. There were 47 red pens in each box. He sold 326 red pens and 471 blue pens. If he had 453 pens left,

(a) how many blue pens did Uncle Ron have left?

(b) how many blue pens were in each box?

27. Gina and Imani have an average of 41 stickers. Gina and Ella have an average of 48 stickers. If Ella has 3 times as many stickers as Gina,

(a) how many stickers does Ella have?

(b) how many more stickers does Imani have than Gina?

Unit 10: PERCENTAGES

Example:

500 people bought tickets to a charity show. 245 of them were men and the rest were women.

What percentage of the people who bought the tickets were women?

Number of women = 500 − 245 = 255

Percentage of people who bought the tickets and were women

$= \dfrac{255}{500} \times 100\%$

$= 51\%$

51% of the people who bought the tickets were women.

Write each percentage as a decimal and a fraction in its simplest form.

		Decimal	Fraction
1.	20%		
2.	45%		
3.	2%		
4.	89%		
5.	72%		

Write each decimal as a percentage.

6. 0.3 = _____

7. 0.05 = _____

8. 0.64 = _____

9. 0.17 = _____

10. 0.94 = _____

11. 0.42 = _____

12. 0.58 = _____

13. 0.23 = _____

14. 0.76 = _____

15. 0.8 = _____

Write each fraction as a percentage.

16. $\frac{1}{2}$ = _____

17. $\frac{9}{10}$ = _____

18. $\frac{16}{25}$ = _____

19. $\frac{18}{200}$ = _____

20. $\frac{240}{400}$ = _____

21. $\frac{3}{4}$ = _____

22. $\frac{2}{5}$ = _____

23. $\frac{11}{20}$ = _____

24. $\frac{59}{100}$ = _____

25. $\frac{350}{500}$ = _____

Solve the following problems. You may use a calculator whenever you see .

26. 20% × 150 = _____

27. 16% × $800 = _____

28. 80% × 55 kg = _____

Singapore Math Practice Level 5B

29. 35% × 220 mi. = _____

30. 40% × $3,300 = _____

31. 88% of 250 = _____

32. 64% of 450 = _____

33. 9% of $1,000 = _____

34. 75% of 600 m = _____

35. 50% of 32 lb. = _____

Write your answers on the lines. You may use a calculator whenever you see .

36. There are 100 apples in a bag. 43 of them are red apples and the rest are green apples. What percentage of the apples are green?

_____

37. Jamie spelled 8 out of 10 words correctly on a spelling test. What percentage of the words did Jamie spell correctly?

_____

38. Marcus had $40. He spent $\frac{1}{4}$ of it and saved the rest. What percentage of the money did Marcus save?

_____

39. There were 300 seats in a movie theater. Only half of the seats were occupied. What percentage of the seats in the theater were occupied?

_____

Singapore Math Practice Level 5B

40. 600 visitors went to the zoo last Sunday. 360 of them were children and the rest were adults. What percentage of the visitors were adults?

_____

41. Rita earns $1,200 a month. She gives 15% of her earnings to her mother. How much does Rita give to her mother?

_____

42. There are 40 students in a class. 35% of them wear glasses. How many students do not wear glasses?

_____

43. A factory produces 800 computers in a week. In order to have a 20% increase in production, how many computers must the factory produce in a week?

_____

44. The original price of a television set was $2,450. It was sold at a discount of 20% during a sale. What was the price of the television set during the sale?

_____

45. Madeline has $4,000 in her savings account. The bank pays 4.5% interest per year. How much interest will Madeline earn after a year?

_____

Singapore Math Practice Level 5B

Solve the following story problems. Show your work in the space below. You may use a calculator whenever you see ▧.

46. The original price of a bicycle was $900. Jiang bought it at a discount of 20%. How much did Jiang pay for the bicycle?

47. Amira, Hannah, and Charlie shared some beads. Amira received 35% of the beads and Hannah received 25% of the beads.

   (a) What percentage of the beads did Charlie receive?

   (b) If Charlie received 600 beads, how many beads did Amira receive?

48. A store owner had 80 kg of rice. He sold 45% of it to Mrs. Philips and 20% of it to Mrs. Sanchez. How much rice did the store owner have left? Write your answer in kilograms.

49. Trevor and his family rented 2 hotel rooms while they were on vacation. The rooms cost them $375, excluding 7% tax. What was the total cost of the hotel rooms?

Singapore Math Practice Level 5B

50. A box contains blue, red, and green pens. 25% of the pens are green and 35% are red. 48 blue pens cannot be used, but the remaining 40% of the blue pens are usable.

(a) How many blue pens are there?

(b) How many pens are there altogether in the box?

51. A farmer has some chicken and duck eggs. 60% of the eggs are chicken eggs, while the rest are duck eggs. There are 420 more chicken eggs than duck eggs.

(a) What percentage more chicken eggs than duck eggs are there?

(b) How many duck eggs does the farmer have?

(c) If each chicken egg is sold for 15 cents and each duck egg is sold for 23 cents, how much money will the farmer make? Write your answer in dollars and cents.

52. Emilia bought a laptop computer at a discount of 15%. The regular price of the computer was $890.

  (a) How much was the computer after the discount?

  (b) If Emilia paid for the computer in 5 monthly installments, how much would she have to pay each month?

53. A man shared $250,000 with his wife and 3 children. His wife received 45% of the money, while his only son received 33% of the money. His 2 daughters shared the rest of the money equally.

  (a) How much did his wife receive?

  (b) How much did his son receive?

  (c) How much did each of his daughters receive?

Singapore Math Practice Level 5B

REVIEW 2

Choose the correct answer, and write its number in the parentheses. You may use a calculator whenever you see 📠**.**

1. Write $\frac{64}{400}$ as a percentage.

    (1) 4%   (3) 16%

    (2) 8%   (4) 64%   (   )

2. Jack spent $815 between January and May. Find Jack's average monthly expenses.

    (1) $136   (3) $3,260

    (2) $163   (4) $4,075   (   )

3. Write 0.03 as a percentage.

    (1) 3%   (3) 33%

    (2) 30%   (4) 300%   (   )

4. A class's average score on a Math test is 72. Find the total score if there are 32 students in the class.

    (1) 104   (3) 2,304

    (2) 1,656   (4) 2,340   (   )

5. After 10% of the visitors had left the museum, there were still 180 visitors. How many visitors were there in the beginning?

    (1) 162   (3) 200

    (2) 198   (4) 220   (   )

6. The sum of 7% of $20 and 60% of $3 is _____.

    (1) $0.40   (3) $12.19

    (2) $3.20   (4) $15.41   (   )

48

7. Which of the following is **not** the same length as the others?

    (1) 20% of 3 yd.   (3) 5% of 12 yd.

    (2) 10% of 6 yd.   (4) 25% of 2 yd.   (   )

Write your answers on the lines. You may use a calculator whenever you see 🖩**.**

8. Write 48% as a fraction in its simplest form.   _____

9. William has 192 books and 48 comic books. What percentage of his books are comics?

                                                            _____

10. Grace is 48 in. tall. Her brother is 8 in. taller than her. What is their average height?

                                                            _____

11. The average height of Calvin, Dmitri, Dante, and Sean is 1.58 m. The average height of these 4 boys, plus Ben and Austin, is 1.6 m. Find the average height of Ben and Austin.

                                                            _____

12. In a band, $\frac{2}{5}$ of the students play the clarinet. What percentage of the students do not play the clarinet?

                                                            _____

13. Tricia saves $315. Her brother saves 20% more than Tricia. Find their average savings.

                                                            _____

14. Vinh bought 4 kg of brown rice and used 65% of it within 3 weeks. How much brown rice did she have left? Write your answer in grams.

                                                            _____

Singapore Math Practice Level 5B

15. The average of 6 numbers is 8.9. The first 4 numbers are 6.5, 3.8, 4.1, and 7.3. Find the total of the 2 remaining numbers.

_____

Solve the following story problems. Show your work in the space below. You may use a calculator whenever you see .

16. The table below shows how Maggie did on her recent tests. The average points on her English and Social Studies tests was 4 more than that on her Math and Science tests.

English	Social Studies	Math	Science
63	74	?	55

(a)   Find the average number of points Maggie received on her Math and Science tests.

(b)   How many points did Maggie receive on her Math test?

Singapore Math Practice Level 5B

17. The average of 5 consecutive numbers is 14. Find the 5 numbers.

18. A factory produces 4,600 pieces of clothing in a month. 35% of these items are shirts. 920 pieces of clothing are shorts and the rest are dresses.

    (a) How many dresses does the factory produce?
    (b) What percentage of the pieces of clothing are dresses?

Singapore Math Practice Level 5B

19. Jonathan is paid $10.20 per hour for working overtime. This is a 20% increase from his normal wage.

   (a) What is his normal hourly wage?
   (b) If Jonathan works 8 regular hours and an hour of overtime in a day, how much does he earn on that day?

20. Jamila has $1,200 in her savings account. The bank pays her 3% interest this year. How much money will Jamila have in her savings account at the end of this year?

Unit 11: ANGLES

1. AOB is a straight line. Find ∠a.

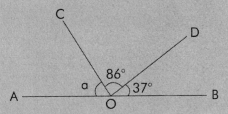

$$\angle a = 180° - 86° - 37°$$
$$= \underline{\textbf{57°}} \text{ (angles on a straight line)}$$

2. Find ∠z.

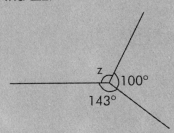

$$\angle z = 360° - 100° - 143°$$
$$= \underline{\textbf{117°}} \text{ (angles at a point)}$$

3. AB and CD are straight lines. Find ∠x, ∠y, and ∠z.

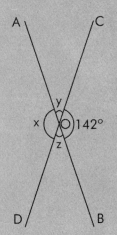

$$\angle x = \angle COB = \underline{\textbf{142°}} \text{ (vertically opposite angles)}$$

$$\angle y = 180° - 142°$$
$$= \underline{\textbf{38°}} \text{ (angles on a straight line)}$$

$$\angle z = \angle y = \underline{\textbf{38°}} \text{ (vertically opposite angles)}$$

Singapore Math Practice Level 5B

Measure each marked angle with a protractor. Write your answers on the lines.

1.

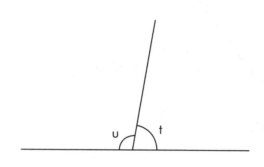

$\angle t = 80°$

$\angle u =$ _____

$\angle t + \angle u =$ _____

2.

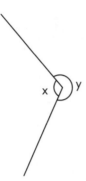

$\angle x = 115°$

$\angle y =$ _____

$\angle x + \angle y =$ _____

3.

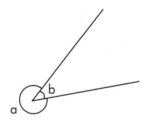

$\angle a = 318°$

$\angle b =$ _____

$\angle a + \angle b =$ _____

Singapore Math Practice Level 5B

4. Measure these marked angles with a protractor. Then, fill in each blank with the correct answer.

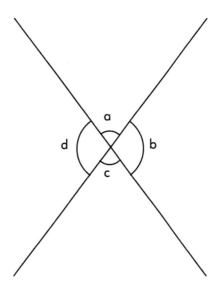

(a) ∠a = _____

   ∠b = _____

   ∠c = _____

   ∠d = _____

(b) ∠a and ∠c are _____ angles.

(c) ∠b and ∠d are _____ angles.

(d) ∠a and ∠b are _____.

(e) ∠a, ∠b, ∠c, and ∠d are _____.

Singapore Math Practice Level 5B

5. Fill in each blank with the correct answer.

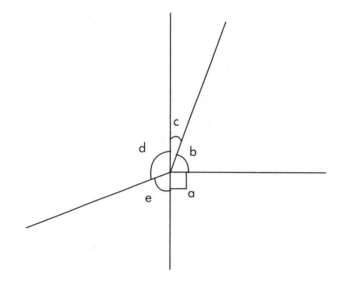

(a) What is the sum of ∠a, ∠b, and ∠c?   _____

(b) Identify the angles on a straight line.   _____

(c) Which two angles can form a right angle?   _____

(d) What is the sum of ∠b, ∠c, ∠d, and ∠e?   _____

Find the unknown angles. Note that each figure is not drawn to scale.

6. AB and CD are straight lines. Find the unknown angles.

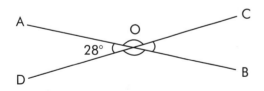

∠AOC = _____

∠DOB = _____

∠COB = _____

Singapore Math Practice Level 5B

7. WOX is a straight line. Find ∠WOY.

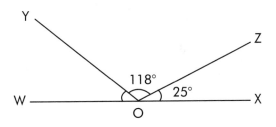

_____

8. AOB is a straight line. Find ∠DOE.

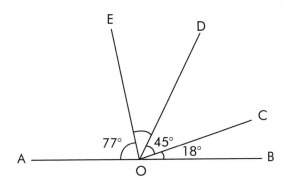

_____

9. SOT is a straight line. Find ∠SOV.

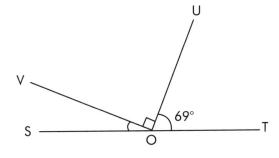

_____

10. Find ∠AOB.

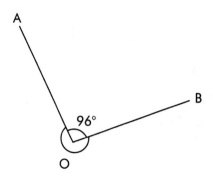

_____

11. Find ∠a.

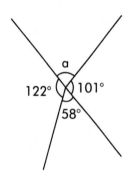

_____

12. Find ∠e.

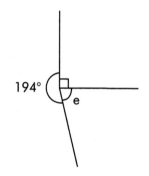

_____

13. Find ∠x.

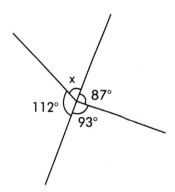

_____

58

14. Find ∠y.

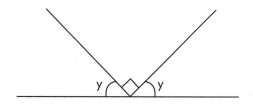

15. Find ∠b and ∠4b.

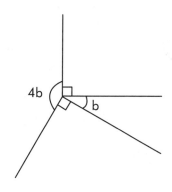

16. Find ∠m.

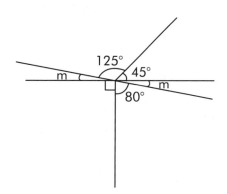

17. Find ∠p and ∠2p.

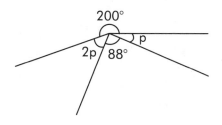

Unit 12: TRIANGLES AND 4-SIDED FIGURES

Examples:

1. XYZ is a right-angled triangle, not drawn to scale. Find ∠XZY.

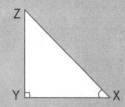

$$\angle XZY = 180° - 90° - 45°$$
$$= \underline{\textbf{45°}} \text{ (sum of ∠s in a triangle = 180°)}$$

2. The figure below is not drawn to scale. Find the unknown marked angles in the trapezoid.

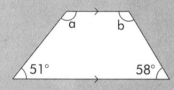

$$\angle a = 180° - 51° = \underline{\textbf{129°}} \text{ (∠s between 2 parallel sides add up to 180°)}$$

$$\angle b = 180° - 58° = \underline{\textbf{122°}} \text{ (∠s between 2 parallel sides add up to 180°)}$$

The figure below is not drawn to scale. Find the unknown marked angles in the parallelogram.

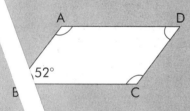

$$\angle ADC = \angle ABC = \underline{\textbf{52°}} \text{ (opp. ∠s are equal)}$$

$$\angle DCB = 180° - 52°$$
$$= \underline{\textbf{128°}} \text{ (∠s between 2 parallel sides add up to 180°)}$$

$$\angle BAD = \angle DCB = \underline{\textbf{128°}} \text{ (opp. ∠s are equal)}$$

4. The figure below is not drawn to scale. Find the unknown marked angles in the rhombus.

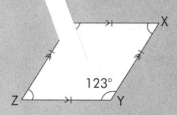

$$\angle ZWX = \angle XYZ = \underline{\textbf{123°}} \text{ (opp. ∠s are equal)}$$

$$\angle WXY = 180° - 123°$$
$$= \underline{\textbf{57°}} \text{ (∠s between 2 parallel sides add up to 180°)}$$

$$\angle WZY = \angle WXY = \underline{\textbf{57°}} \text{ (opp. ∠s are equal)}$$

Singapore Math Practice Level 5B

Find each unknown angle. Note that the triangles are not drawn to scale.

1. Find ∠ABC.

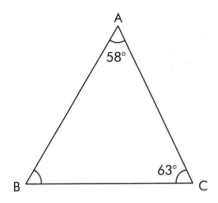

    ∠ABC = _____

2. Find ∠YXZ.

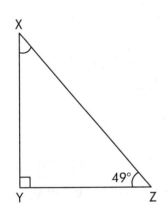

    ∠YXZ = _____

3. Find ∠NLM.

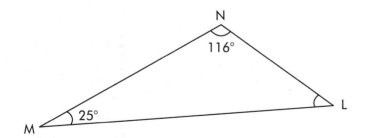

    ∠NLM = _____

Singapore Math Practice Level 5B

4. In triangle ABC, AB = BC and ∠ABC = 42°. Find ∠ACB.

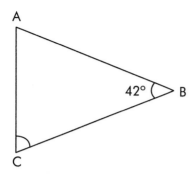

∠ACB = _____

5. In triangle EFG, EH = EF, ∠EGF = 53°, and ∠GEF = 59°. Find ∠EHF.

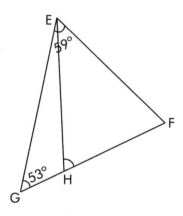

∠EHF = _____

6. In equilateral triangle PQR, ∠QPS = 24°. Find ∠PSR.

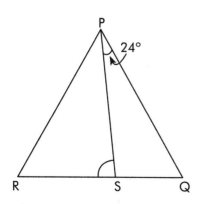

∠PSR = _____

7. In triangle ABC, DB = DC and ∠DCB = 31°. Find ∠ADC.

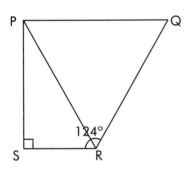

∠ADC = _____

8. PSR is a right-angled triangle and PQR is an equaliteral triangle. ∠SRQ is 124°. Find ∠SPR.

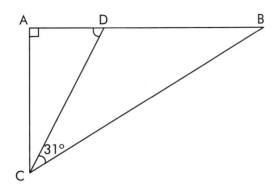

∠SPR = _____

9. In triangle ABC, AB = AC and ∠BAC = 124°. In triangle BDE, ∠BED = 90° and ∠EDB = 59°. Find ∠ABD.

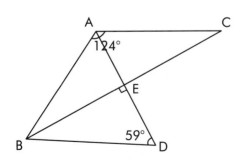

∠ABD = _____

Singapore Math Practice Level 5B

Find each unknown marked angle. Note that the figures are not drawn to scale. Write your answers on the lines provided in the box. Identify the type of triangle by putting a check mark (✓) in the correct box.

10.

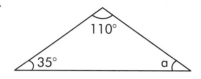

13.

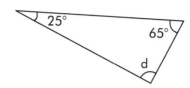

11.

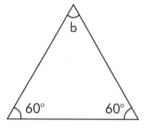

14.

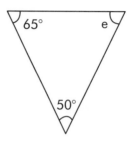

12.

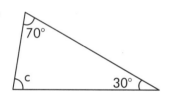

15.

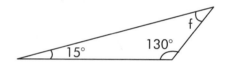

	Angles	Isosceles triangle	Equilateral triangle	Right-angled triangle
10.	∠a = _____ °			
11.	∠b = _____ °			
12.	∠c = _____ °			
13.	∠d = _____ °			
14.	∠e = _____ °			
15.	∠f = _____ °			

Singapore Math Practice Level 5B

Find each unknown marked angle. Note that the following 4-sided figures are not drawn to scale.

16.

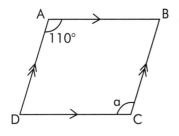

$\angle a = \underline{\hspace{3cm}}$

17.

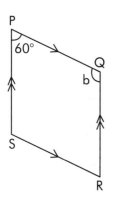

$\angle b = \underline{\hspace{3cm}}$

18.

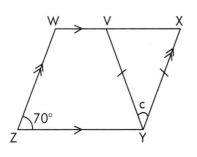

$\angle c = \underline{\hspace{3cm}}$

19.

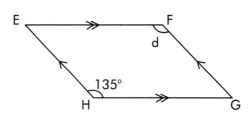

$\angle d = \underline{\hspace{3cm}}$

20.

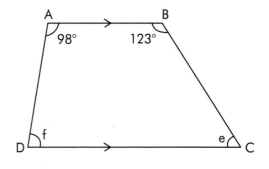

$\angle e = \underline{\hspace{3cm}}$

$\angle f = \underline{\hspace{3cm}}$

21.

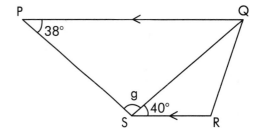

$\angle g = \underline{\hspace{3cm}}$

Singapore Math Practice Level 5B

22.

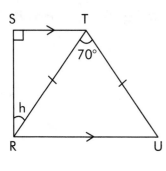

∠h = _____

23.

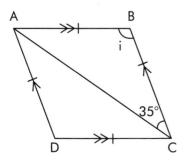

∠i = _____

24.

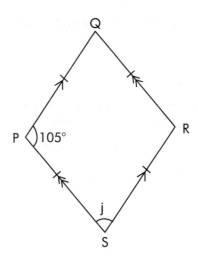

∠j = _____

25.

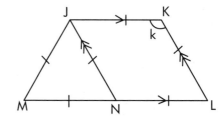

∠k = _____

26. The figure below is a trapezoid where PS // QR. Find ∠PSR.

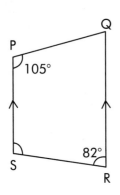

∠PSR = _____

27. ABCD is a parallelogram where ∠BAD = 118° and ∠BCA = 68°. Find ∠ACD.

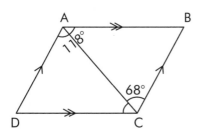

∠ACD = _____

28. WXYZ is a parallelogram where ∠WZX = 90°, ∠ZXY = 90°, and ∠ZWX = 61°. Find ∠WXZ, ∠XZY, and ∠XYZ.

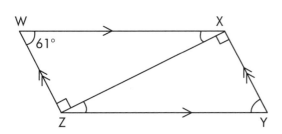

∠WXZ = _____

∠XZY = _____

∠XYZ = _____

29. ABCD is a rhombus where ∠ABC = 68° and ∠BAC = 57°. Find ∠CAD.

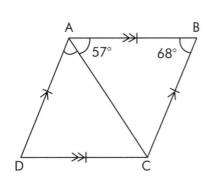

∠CAD = _____

Singapore Math Practice Level 5B

30. OPQR is a parallelogram where ∠ROP = 70°, ∠OPR = 47°, and ∠RQS = 32°. Find ∠PQS and ∠QRS.

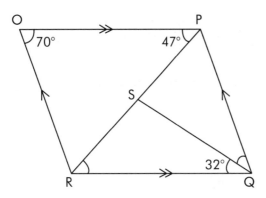

∠PQS = _____

∠QRS = _____

31. WXYZ is a parallelogram where ∠ZWY = 70°, ∠XZY = 30°, and ∠ZYX = 115°. Find ∠YWX and ∠WXZ.

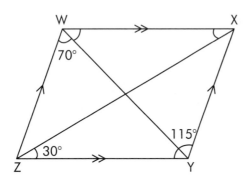

∠YWX = _____

∠WXZ = _____

Singapore Math Practice Level 5B

REVIEW 3

Choose the correct answer, and write its number in the parentheses.

1. Which of the following is a rhombus?

(1)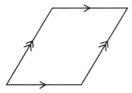

(3)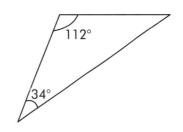

(2)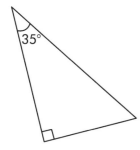

(4)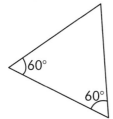

(   )

2. Which of the following figures is an isosceles triangle?

(1)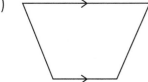

(3)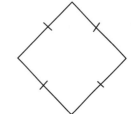

(2)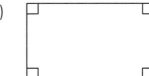

(4)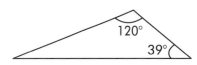

(   )

Singapore Math Practice Level 5B

Note that the following figures are not drawn to scale.

3. In triangle ABC, AB = BC and ∠BAC = 62°. Find ∠ABC.

   (1) 56°
   (2) 62°
   (3) 118°
   (4) 124°

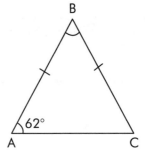

(   )

4. In triangle WXY, WX = XZ = WZ and ∠WYX = 35°. Find ∠ZXY.

   (1) 25°
   (2) 55°
   (3) 60°
   (4) 120°

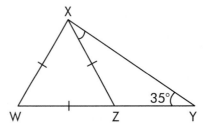

(   )

5. The figure below is a parallelogram. What is the value of ∠d?

   (1) 43°
   (2) 47°
   (3) 57°
   (4) 133°

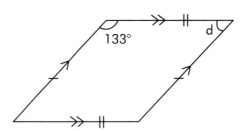

(   )

Singapore Math Practice Level 5B

Use the figure below to answer Questions 6 and 7.

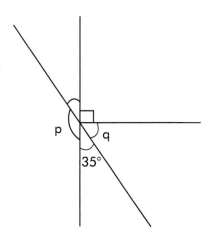

6. Find ∠p.

    (1) 35°   (3) 145°
    (2) 90°   (4) 180°   (   )

7. Find the sum of ∠p and ∠q.

    (1) 55°   (3) 80°
    (2) 145°   (4) 200°   (   )

Write your answers on the lines. Note that the figures are not drawn to scale.

8. In triangle ADE, AE = ED = DA. In triangle CDE, CD = DE and ∠CDE = 120°. In triangle BCE, ∠BCE is 19°. Find ∠EBC.

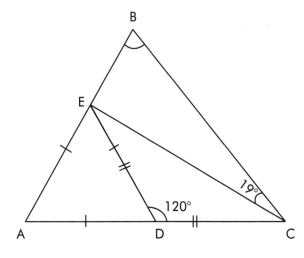

_____

Singapore Math Practice Level 5B

9. PQRS is a rhombus where ∠SPQ = 137°. Find the sum of ∠SRQ and ∠PQR.

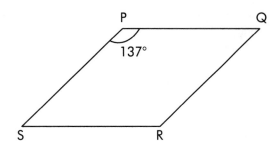

_____

10. In the figure below, CDEF is a trapezoid, where CF // DE and ∠CFE = 116°. In triangle CDE, CD = DE and ∠DCE = 58°. Find ∠CEF.

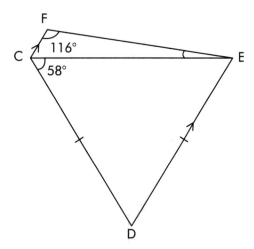

_____

11. The figure below is made of 2 equilateral triangles. Find the sum of the 6 unknown angles.

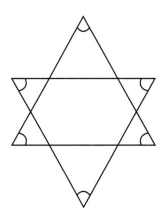

_____

12. PQRS is a rhombus. ∠SPQ = 104°. Find ∠QRS.

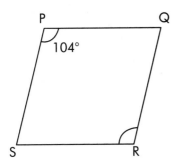

_____

13. Find the sum of ∠EOF and ∠AOB by measuring them with a protractor.

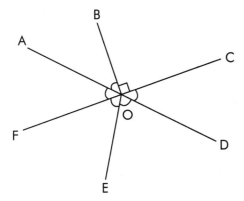

_____

14. STUV is a trapezoid where ST // VU, ∠VST = 79°, and ∠STU = 71°. UVWX is a trapezoid where VU // WX. Find ∠VWX and ∠VUX.

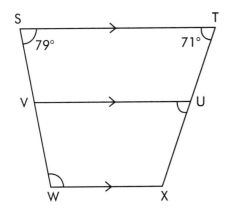

_____

Singapore Math Practice Level 5B

15. Find ∠4b.

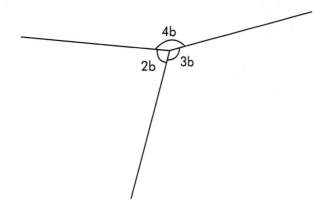

16. Find the sum of ∠a and ∠c.

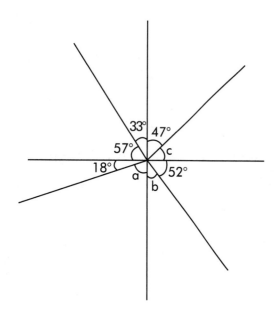

74

17. The figure below is made of 2 triangles. ABC is an equilateral triangle. ABD is an isosceles triangle. Find ∠x.

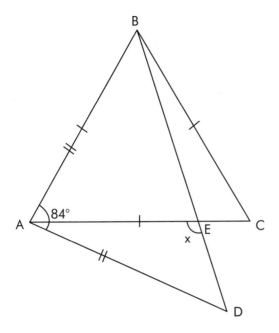

18. PQRT is a trapezoid where PQ // TR and ∠QRT = 72°. PST is an equilateral triangle where PS = ST = TP. PQT is an isosceles triangle where PT = PQ. Find ∠a.

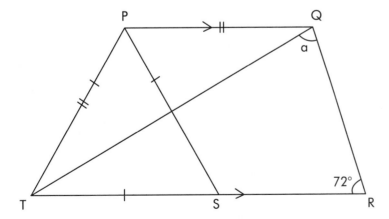

Singapore Math Practice Level 5B

19. Find ∠4a.

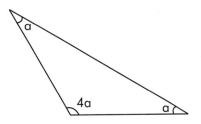

20. In rhombus ABCD, AB = BC = CD = DA, AB // DC, and AD // BC. In triangle BCE, BC = CE and ∠BCE = 42°. Find ∠BCD.

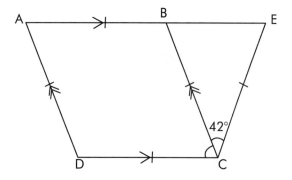

Singapore Math Practice Level 5B

Unit 13: GEOMETRICAL CONSTRUCTION

Example:

Draw a triangle ABC in which AB is 3 cm, ∠CAB = 80°, and ∠ACB = 48°.

Step 1: Draw Line AB 3 cm using a ruler.

Step 2: Measure and draw an 80° angle at Point A using a protractor.

Step 3: Measure and draw a 48° angle at Point C. Draw a line from Point C to Point B.

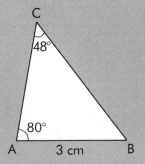

1.   Draw a triangle ABC in which AB = 6 cm, ∠CAB = 80°, and ∠CBA = 45°.

Singapore Math Practice Level 5B

2. Draw a triangle EFG with the given measurements.

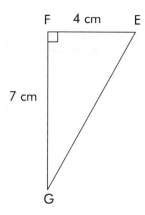

3. Draw a parallelogram ABCD in which AB = 5 cm, AC = 3 cm, and ABC = 60°.

Singapore Math Practice Level 5B

4. Draw a square OPQR in which each side measures 4.5 cm.

5. Draw a rectangle WXYZ with the given measurements.

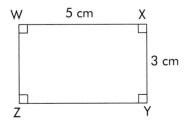

Singapore Math Practice Level 5B

6. Draw a rhombus EFGH in which each side measure 3.5 cm and ∠EFG = 70°.

7. Draw a trapezoid CDEF in which CD // EF, CE = 6 cm, EF = 7 cm, ∠CEF = 50°, and ∠DFE = 75°.

Unit 14: VOLUME

Examples:

1. Find the volume of a cube whose edge is 8 in.

   Volume = Edge × Edge × Edge

   $= 8 \times 8 \times 8$

   $= 512 \text{ in.}^3$

   The volume of the cube is __512 in.³__.

2. Find the volume of a cuboid with length 11 cm, width 13 cm, and height 7 cm.

   Volume = Length × Width × Height

   $= 11 \times 13 \times 7$

   $= 1{,}001 \text{ cm}^3$

   The volume of the cuboid is __1,001 cm³__.

Singapore Math Practice Level 5B

Write down the correct number of unit cubes used to build the solids shown below.

1.

   Solid A

   Number of unit cubes used to build Solid A = _____

2.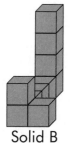

   Solid B

   Number of unit cubes used to build Solid B = _____

3.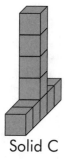

   Solid C

   Number of unit cubes used to build Solid C = _____

Draw the following figures on the dot grid.

4.

5.

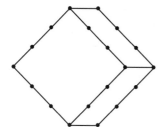

Complete the following drawings.

6.

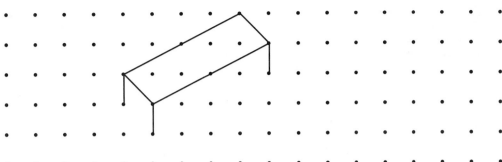

7.

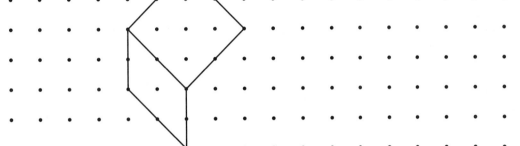

8.

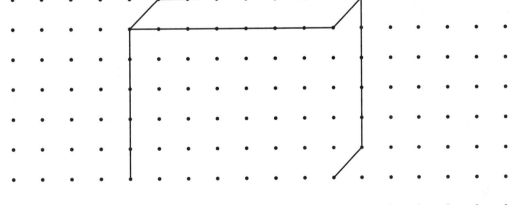

Singapore Math Practice Level 5B

The solids shown below are made of 1-cm cubes. Fill in each blank with the correct answer.

9.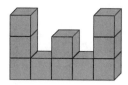

Volume = _____

10.

Volume = _____

11.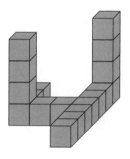

Volume = _____

12.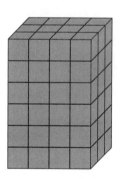

Length = _____

Width = _____

Height = _____

Volume = _____

13.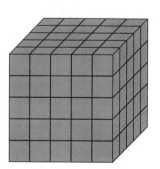

Length = _____

Width = _____

Height = _____

Volume = _____

Singapore Math Practice Level 5B

Find the length, width, height, and volume of each cube or cuboid. You may use a calculator whenever you see 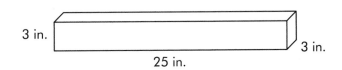**.**

14.

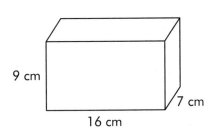

Length = _____

Width = _____

Height = _____

Volume = _____

15.

Length = _____

Width = _____

Height = _____

Volume = _____

Singapore Math Practice Level 5B

16.

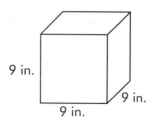

9 in.

9 in.

9 in.

Edge   = _____

Volume = _____

 17.

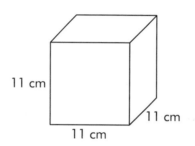

11 cm

11 cm

11 cm

Edge   = _____

Volume = _____

Find the volume of these cubes and cuboids. You may use a calculator whenever you see 🖩**.**

18.

Length	Width	Height
10 in.	8 in.	12 in.

Volume = _____

19.

Length	Width	Height
4 cm	5 cm	18 cm

Volume = _____

20.

Edge
15 ft.

Volume = _____

21.

Length	Width	Height
3 cm	3 cm	9 cm

Volume = _____

22.

Edge
26 in.

Volume = _____

Write the following in cubic centimeters.

23. 315 mL   = _____

24. 1 L 200 mL = _____

25. 19 L 3 mL = _____

26. 59 mL   = _____

27. 43 L 7 mL = _____

28. 20 L 88 mL = _____

Write the following in liters and milliliters.

29. 755 cm³   = _____

30. 3,004 cm³ = _____

31. 5,060 cm³ = _____

32. 75,070 cm³ = _____

33. 14,005 cm³ = _____

34. 48,276 cm³ = _____

Solve the following story problems. Show your work in the space below. You may use a calculator whenever you see **.**

35. A rectangular tank measures 13 in. by 25 in. by 12 in. Find its capacity.

36. The edge of a cube is 13 cm. Find its volume in cubic meters.

37. A cuboid is 38 in. long, 17 in. wide, and 9.5 in. high. Find its volume.

Singapore Math Practice Level 5B

38. A rectangular tank with a base area of 600 cm² and a height of 19 cm is half-filled with water. Find how much water is needed to fill the tank completely. Write your answer in liters.
(1 L = 1,000 cm³)

39. Xavier wants to completely fill a cube-shaped tank that has an edge of 24 cm. He pours bottles of water with a capacity of 384 mL into the tank, one at a time. How many bottles of water will he need to fill the tank completely?

Singapore Math Practice Level 5B

40. A tank 30 cm long, 12.5 cm wide, and 20 cm high is $\frac{3}{4}$ filled with water. A tap is turned on for 3 minutes to fill the tank completely. (1 L = 1,000 cm³)

   (a) How much water is needed to fill the tank to its brim? Write your answer in liters.

   (b) Find the amount of water that flows from the tap per minute.

41. A fish pond measures 70 in. by 90 in. by 110 in. It needs another 5,880 in.³ of water to fill it completely. Find the volume of water in the fish pond.

42. A tank measuring 48 in. by 38 in. by 28 in. is 75% filled with water. How much water will be needed to fill the tank to its brim?

43. A bucket can hold 1.5 L of water. A beaker is 5 cm long, 5 cm wide, and 6 cm high. How many beakers of water are needed to fill the bucket? Assume the beakers are completely filled with water. (1 L = 1,000 cm³)

44. $\frac{2}{3}$ of the tank shown below is filled with water.

    (a) Find the volume of water in the tank.

    (b) If a block of ice, 13 in. by 16 in. by 9 in., is lowered into the tank, find the new volume of water in the tank when the block of ice melts completely.

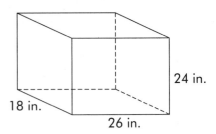

18 in.

24 in.

26 in.

5. Ethan turns on a tap to fill a tank with water. The tank has a square base that measures 40 cm per side and a height of 41.25 cm. Water from the tap flows into the tank at a rate of 4.5 liters per minute. How long should Ethan let the water run if he wants to fill $\frac{3}{4}$ of the tank?
(1 L = 1,000 cm³)

Singapore Math Practice Level 5B

REVIEW 4

Choose the correct answer, and write its number in the parentheses. You may use a calculator whenever you see .

1. Write 4 L 325 mL in cubic centimeters. (1 L = 1,000 cm³)

   (1)   4.325 cm³   (3)   432.5 cm³

   (2)   43.25 cm³   (4)   4,325 cm³   (   )

2. A cube has a base area of 64 in.². What is its volume?

   (1)   256 in.³   (3)   1,024 in.³

   (2)   512 in.³   (4)   4,096 in.³   (   )

3. Find the number of unit cubes used to build the solid shown below.

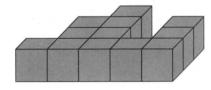

   (1)   10   (3)   12

   (2)   11   (4)   13   (   )

4. A rectangular tank measures 24 in. by 13 in. by 7 in. Find the capacity of the tank.

   (1)   2,048 in.³   (3)   2,148 in.³

   (2)   2,118 in.³   (4)   2,184 in.³   (   )

5. Write 10,040 cm³ in liters and milliliters.

   (1)   10 L 4 mL   (3)   100 L 4 mL

   (2)   10 L 40 mL   (4)   100 L 40 mL   (   )

Singapore Math Practice Level 5B

6. Which of the following best describes the figure shown below?

    (1) ABCD is a parallelogram.
    (2) ABCD is a square.
    (3) ABCD is a rhombus.
    (4) ABCD is a trapezoid.   (   )

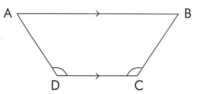

7. A tank, 18 in. by 12 in. by 10 in., is $\frac{3}{4}$ filled with water. How much more water is needed to fill the tank completely?

    (1) 540 in.³   (3) 2,140 in.³
    (2) 1,620 in.³   (4) 5,400 in.³   (   )

8. Jessica fills a cube-shaped tank that has an edge of 70 cm with water from a tap. Water flows into the tank at a rate of 7 L per minute. How long will it take to fill the tank completely?
    (1 L = 1,000 cm³)

    (1) 10 min.   (3) 70 min.
    (2) 49 min.   (4) 100 min.   (   )

Write your answers on the lines. You may use a calculator whenever you see .

9. The figure below is a parallelogram. AB = 5 cm and BC = 3 cm. Find ∠ABC.

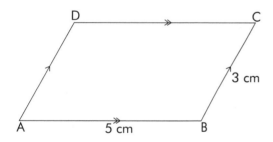

    _____

10. The solid below is made of 1-in. cubes. Find the volume of the solid.

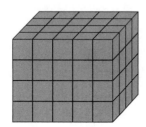

    _____

Singapore Math Practice Level 5B

11. Write 12,012 mL in cubic centimeters. _____

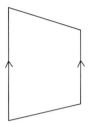12. Find the capacity of a rectangular tank 16 in. by 18 in. by 11 in.

_____

13. Identify the figure shown below.

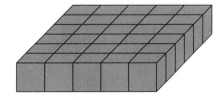

_____

14. James is drawing a 4-sided figure. Below are the properties of the 4-sided figure.

- It has 4 equal sides.
- Its opposite sides are equal.
- Its opposite angles are equal.

What 4-sided figure is James drawing? _____

15. A container has a square base of 121 cm² and a height of 8 cm. It is $\frac{1}{4}$ filled with water. The water is then poured into cups of 22 mL. How many cups are needed to contain the volume of water in the container?

_____

16. The solid below is made of 1-in. cubes.

What is its height if the volume of the solid is 30 in.³? _____

Singapore Math Practice Level 5B

Solve the following story problems. Show your work in the space below. You may use a calculator whenever you see 🖩**.**

17. Draw a square EFGH that measures 3.5 cm per side.

18. A rectangular tank, 45 in. long, 24 in. wide, and 30 in. high, is filled with water. Maggie takes $\frac{1}{5}$ of the water from the tank. How much water does she take?

Singapore Math Practice Level 5B

19. Draw a parallelogram WXYZ in which WX = 4 cm, XY = 3 cm, and ∠XWZ = 50°.

20. A container with a base area of 896 cm² and a height of 22 cm is half-filled with water. If a cup of 44 cm³ is used to scoop the water out of the container, how many times must the cup be used to empty the water from the container?

FINAL REVIEW

Choose the correct answer, and write its number in the parentheses. Do not use a calculator.

1. A tap runs at a rate of 550 cm³ per minute. How many liters of water can be collected when the tap runs for half an hour? (1 L = 1,000 cm³)

    (1) 1.65 L   (3) 165 L

    (2) 16.5 L   (4) 16,500 L   (   )

2. The figure below is not drawn to scale. AB is a straight line. ∠BOC = 63° and ∠AOD is a right-angle. Find ∠DOC.

    (1) 27°

    (2) 90°

    (3) 117°

    (4) 153°

    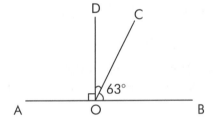

    (   )

3. ABCD is a rhombus. BCE is a triangle. Find ∠x.

    (1) 26°

    (2) 52°

    (3) 104°

    (4) 128°

    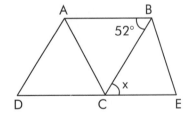

    (   )

4. Which of the following is not a property of a rhombus?

    (1) Each pair of angles between the perpendicular sides of a rhombus adds up to 180°.

    (2) The opposite angles in a rhombus are equal.

    (3) The opposite sides in a rhombus are parallel.

    (4) All sides in a rhombus are equal.   (   )

Singapore Math Practice Level 5B

5. The volume of water in the tank shown below is _____.

    (1) 260 in.³
    (2) 480 in.³
    (3) 780 in.³
    (4) 1,040 in.³

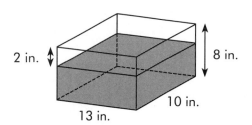

    (   )

6. ABC and ADE are triangles. ∠BAC = 20° and ∠BCE = 125°. Find ∠CBD.

    (1) 55°
    (2) 75°
    (3) 105°
    (4) 125°

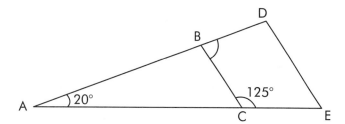

    (   )

7. Convert 8.052 L to liters and milliliters.

    (1) 8 L 52 mL   (3) 8 L 520 mL
    (2) 8 L 502 mL   (4) 80 L 52 mL   (   )

8. AB and CD are straight lines. Find the sum of ∠a and ∠c. The figure below is not drawn scale.

    (1) 76°
    (2) 93°
    (3) 104°
    (4) 145°

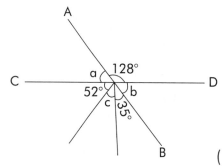

    (   )

9. Simon bought a computer for $561.75, including 7%. tax. How much was the computer without tax?

    (1) $500   (3) $555
    (2) $525   (4) $561   (   )

Singapore Math Practice Level 5B

10. The figure below is not drawn to scale. Find ∠a.

(1)   27°
(2)   50°
(3)   57°
(4)   67°

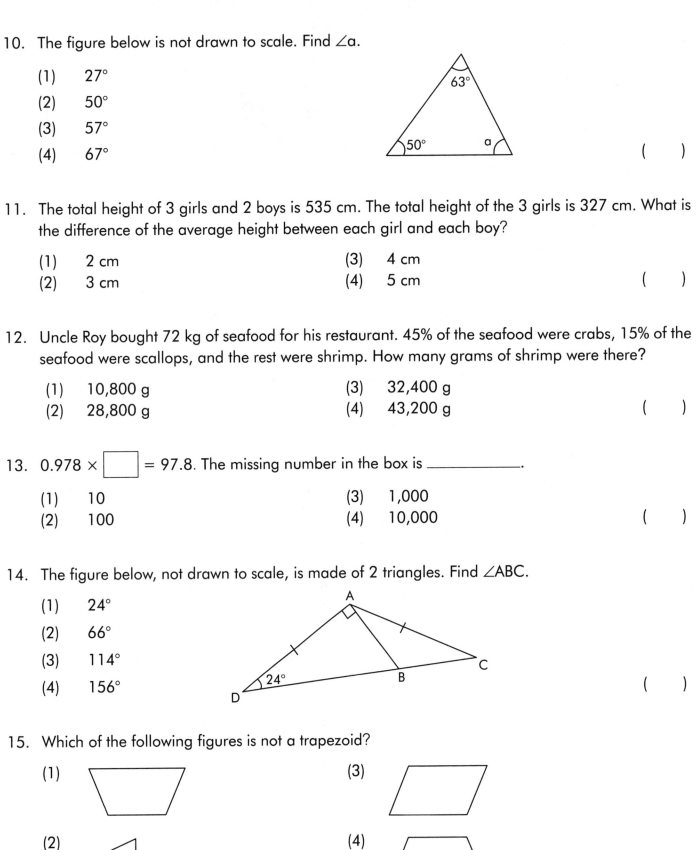

(   )

11. The total height of 3 girls and 2 boys is 535 cm. The total height of the 3 girls is 327 cm. What is the difference of the average height between each girl and each boy?

(1)   2 cm   (3)   4 cm
(2)   3 cm   (4)   5 cm

(   )

12. Uncle Roy bought 72 kg of seafood for his restaurant. 45% of the seafood were crabs, 15% of the seafood were scallops, and the rest were shrimp. How many grams of shrimp were there?

(1)   10,800 g   (3)   32,400 g
(2)   28,800 g   (4)   43,200 g

(   )

13. 0.978 × ☐ = 97.8. The missing number in the box is _____.

(1)   10   (3)   1,000
(2)   100   (4)   10,000

(   )

14. The figure below, not drawn to scale, is made of 2 triangles. Find ∠ABC.

(1)   24°
(2)   66°
(3)   114°
(4)   156°

(   )

15. Which of the following figures is not a trapezoid?

(1)

(3)

(2)

(4)

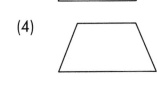

(   )

Singapore Math Practice Level 5B

Write your answers on the lines.

16. $104 \div 1,000 =$ _____   _____

17. Kaitlyn bought 13 yd. of fabric to make some dresses. A yard of fabric costs $2.99. How much did she spend?

_____

18. Write 0.02 as a percentage.

19. The average mass of Luis, Ian, and Lucy is 42 kg.
    The average mass of Luis, Lucy, and Will is 45 kg.
    If Luis's mass is 36 kg and Lucy's mass is 40 kg, find the total mass of Ian and Will.

_____

20. Aliyah spends 54% of her birthday money. If she receives $60 for her birthday, how much does she spend?

_____

21. Mrs. Spencer makes 1.8 liters of iced tea every day. If she makes the same amount of iced tea for 2 weeks, how much tea does she make altogether? Write your answer in milliliters.

_____

22. The figure below is not drawn to scale. Find ∠OQP. Identify what type of triangle OPQ is.

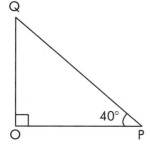

_____

Singapore Math Practice Level 5B

23. RST is a triangle, not drawn to scale. ∠TSU = 82° and ∠SUR = 144°.
Find ∠STU.

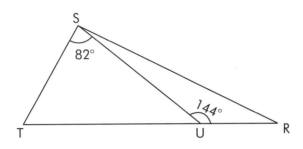

_____

24. The capacity of a bathtub is 40 gal. When it is only 30% filled with water, how much more water is needed to fill the bathtub completely?

_____

25. Complete the drawing of the cuboid below.

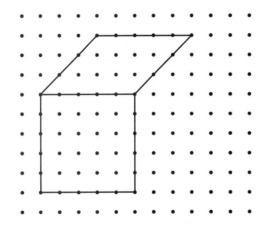

26. Kimiko earns $1,440 a month by teaching part-time at a college. If she teaches 20 hours a month, what is her average hourly pay?

_____

27. Write 52% as a fraction in its simplest form.

_____

28. The total age of 3 children is 19 years 3 months. What is their average age? Write your answer in years and months.

_____

Singapore Math Practice Level 5B

29. Deshawn invests $12,500 in a fund. The interest rate is 8.5% per year. How much will he have in the fund after a year?

_____

30. ABCD is a parallelogram, not drawn to scale. ∠BAD = 27° and ∠ADB = 65°. Find ∠DBC.

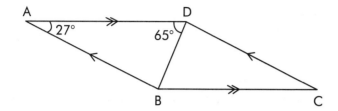

_____

Write your answers on the lines. You may use a calculator.

31. There are 6,055 students in a school. 3,633 of them are girls. What percentage of the students are boys?

_____

32. A blue pen costs $1.95. Find the total cost of 20 dozen identical blue pens.

_____

33. Find the volume of a cube whose edge is 36 cm.

_____

34. Divide 3,120.75 by 15.

_____

35. Find the value of 32.05 × 13.

_____

Singapore Math Practice Level 5B

36. There are 900 students in a school. 720 of the students take Spanish. 0.75 of the remaining students take French and the rest take Latin. How many students take Latin?

37. The figure below, not drawn to scale, is made of a parallelogram and a triangle. ∠GFJ = 68° and ∠FJG = 48°. Find ∠EFG.

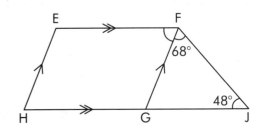

38. The figure below, not drawn to scale, is made of an isosceles triangle SQR and an equilaterial triangle PQR. ∠RSQ = 134°. Find ∠SQP.

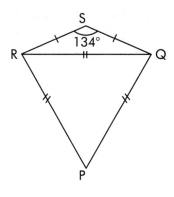

39. During weekdays, a museum has an average of 790 visitors per day. During weekends, the total number of visitors is 2,910. What is the average number of visitors per day during the course of an entire week?

Singapore Math Practice Level 5B

40. Anna bought a small boat that cost $2,999 and a trailer for $699. She paid 7% in tax for the 2 items.

    (a)   How much money did she pay in tax?
    (b)   How much did she pay altogether?

41. Draw a trapezoid ABCD in which AD // BC, AB = 2 cm, BC = 7 cm, $\angle ABC = 44°$, and $\angle BCD = 38°$.

Singapore Math Practice Level 5B

42. Eli spends 20% of his salary on food and spends another 32% on housing. If he has spent $585 on food and housing, how much is Eli's salary?

43. The owner of a store had a sack of flour that weighed 60 kg. He sold 0.45 of the flour to Mr. Romero and $\frac{33}{100}$ of the flour to Mrs. Drew. After selling flour to both of them, he packed the remaining flour into bags weighing 120 g. How many 120-g bags of flour did he pack?

Singapore Math Practice Level 5B

44. Henry earns $12.40 per hour if he works at least 8 hours a day. He earns 1.5 times his normal hourly rate for every additional hour he works in a day. How much does Henry earn if he works 10 hours each day for 5 days?

45. A tank measuring 35 in. by 19 in. by 31 in. is filled with some water. Find the volume of water needed to fill the tank completely.

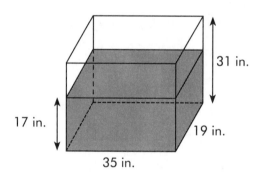

Singapore Math Practice Level 5B

46. It took Meghan 12 minutes to draw 4 patterns on some fabric. How many patterns could she have drawn in 9 hours and 36 minutes?

47. A machine can pack 200 bars of soap in 5 minutes. How many bars of soap can the machine pack in 1.5 hours?

48. Jimmy has a tank 80 cm long, 60 cm wide, and 120 cm high. Water flows into the tank for $1\frac{1}{2}$ hours at a rate of 1.6 liters per minute. (1 L = 1,000 cm³)

(a) How much water will be in the tank after $1\frac{1}{2}$ hours? Write your answer in cubic centimeters.

(b) How many hours will it take for the tank to be completely filled?

CHALLENGE QUESTIONS

Solve the following problems on another sheet of paper.

1. The average of 4 different numbers is 4.4. Each number is bigger than one of the other numbers by 1.1. Find the smallest number.

2. Y is a number between 5 and 20. When Y is divided by 2, 3, and 6, it will have a remainder of 1. What are the possible values of Y?

3. I am a 4-digit number.

   (a) My first digit is the greatest odd number and is the sum of my second and third digits.

   (b) My last digit is 60% of my third digit.

   (c) My second digit is the only even number.

   (d) The sum of my 4 digits is 21.

   What am I?

4. X is a number between 70 and 100. When X is divided by 3, it has a remainder of 1. When X is divided by 6, it has a remainder of 1. What is the greatest possible value of X?

5. Mr. Whitney bought 6 tennis rackets and a basketball for $390. Mr. Jackson bought 3 tennis rackets and an basketball for $225. How much did the tennis rackets and the basketball cost?

6. In order to win the grand prize, Ben has to crack this secret code. Use the clues to help Ben to crack the code.

   $$8 \ 3 \ \_\_ \ \_\_ \ 6 \ 5$$

   (a) The third digit is greater than the second digit.
   (b) The difference is 3 when the third digit is subtracted from the fourth digit.
   (c) When the sum of all the numbers is divided by 5, it has a remainder of 3.
   (d) When the sum of all the numbers is divided by 6, it has a remainder of 3.

7. Sunita bought some stickers. The number of stickers could be distributed equally among 6, 8, or 12 children. If the number of stickers was between 40 and 60, how many stickers did Sunita buy?

8. I am a 7-digit number. Given the clues below, what am I?
   (a) The last digit is the smallest whole number.
   (b) The first digit is an even number and a product of the third and fifth digits.
   (c) The second digit is an odd number and the difference between the fourth and sixth digits.
   (d) The sum of all the digits is 32.
   (e) The sum of the first 3 digits is the same as the sum of the last 3 digits.
   (f) All the digits are different.

9. When Number Z is divided by 5, its quotient is a multiple of 3. The sum of the quotient and 3 is 24. The difference of the quotient and 3 is 18. Find Number Z.

10. Aunt Elena made some orange juice. She gave 30% of the orange juice to her neighbors. Her children drank $\frac{11}{10}$ more juice than the amount of juice she gave her neighbors. If there was 315 mL of orange juice left, how much orange juice did Aunt Elena make?

11. The average of 3 different numbers is $36\frac{1}{3}$. The second number is $\frac{2}{5}$ more than the first number. The third number is $\frac{2}{5}$ more than the second number. Find the largest number.

12. 20 pizzas and a box of chicken wings cost $227.90. 18 pizzas and a box of chicken wings cost $206.10. How much are 4 pizzas and 4 boxes of chicken wings?

Unit 7: More On Decimals

1. $0.5 = \frac{5}{10} = \frac{1}{2}$

2. $6.9 = \mathbf{6\frac{9}{10}}$

3. $46.6 = 46\frac{6}{10} = \mathbf{46\frac{3}{5}}$

4. $258.3 = \mathbf{258\frac{3}{10}}$

5. $0.02 = \frac{2}{100} = \frac{1}{50}$

6. $7.36 = 7\frac{36}{100} = 7\frac{18}{50} = \mathbf{7\frac{9}{25}}$

7. $69.15 = 69\frac{15}{100} = \mathbf{69\frac{3}{20}}$

8. $420.07 = \mathbf{420\frac{7}{100}}$

9. $0.003 = \frac{3}{\mathbf{1,000}}$

10. $8.802 = 8\frac{802}{1,000} = \mathbf{8\frac{401}{500}}$

11. $59.575 = 59\frac{575}{1,000} = \mathbf{59\frac{23}{40}}$

12. $952.007 = \mathbf{952}\frac{7}{\mathbf{1,000}}$

13. $0.5 \times 10 = \mathbf{5}$

14. $44.9 \times 10 = \mathbf{449}$

15. $105.67 \times 10 = \mathbf{1,056.7}$

16. $26.093 \times 10 = \mathbf{260.93}$

17. $0.08 \times 100 = \mathbf{8}$

18. $37.71 \times 100 = \mathbf{3,771}$

19. $480.409 \times 100 = \mathbf{48,040.9}$

20. $0.28 \times 1,000 = \mathbf{280}$

21. $184.6 \times 1,000 = \mathbf{184,600}$

22. $475.36 \times 1,000 = \mathbf{475,360}$

23. $3.2 = 0.32 \times \mathbf{10}$

24. $70 = 0.7 \times \mathbf{100}$

25. $9,001 = 90.01 \times \mathbf{100}$

26. $\mathbf{0.148} \times 10 = 1.48$

27. $\mathbf{0.065} \times 100 = 6.5$

28. $\mathbf{0.5} \times 1,000 = 500$

29. $0.2 \times \mathbf{4} \times 10 = 8$

30. $68.35 \times \mathbf{9} \times 10 = \mathbf{6,151.5}$

31. $9.4 \times 3 \times 100 = \mathbf{2,820}$

32. $204.56 \times \mathbf{7} \times \mathbf{100} = \mathbf{143,192}$

33. $50.9 \times 6 \times 1,000 = \mathbf{305,400}$

34. $74.21 \times \mathbf{3} \times 1,000 = \mathbf{222,630}$

35. $\mathbf{121.5} \times 10 = \mathbf{12.15} \times 100$
$\quad = \mathbf{1.215} \times 1,000$

36. $484.9 \times \mathbf{10} = 48.49 \times \mathbf{100}$
$\quad = 4.849 \times \mathbf{1,000}$

37. $\mathbf{1,200.8} \times 10 = \mathbf{120.08} \times 100$
$\quad = \mathbf{12.008} \times 1,000$

38. $7 \div 10 = \mathbf{0.7}$

39. $0.9 \div 10 = \mathbf{0.09}$

40. $95.73 \div 10 = \mathbf{9.573}$

41. $78.7 \div 100 = \mathbf{0.787}$

42. $5,461 \div 100 = \mathbf{54.61}$

43. $1,003 \div 1,000 = \mathbf{1.003}$

44. $20,120 \div 1,000 = \mathbf{20.12}$

45. $7.162 = 71.62 \div \mathbf{10}$

46. $1.879 = 187.9 \div \mathbf{100}$

47. $0.807 = \mathbf{807} \div \mathbf{1,000}$

48. $0.218 = \mathbf{2.18} \div 10$

49. $3.649 = \mathbf{364.9} \div 100$

50. $0.092 = \mathbf{92} \div 1,000$

51. $13.55 = \mathbf{13,550} \div 1,000$

52. $2.4 \div 2 \div 10 = \mathbf{0.12}$

53. $4.05 \div 5 \div 10 = \mathbf{0.081}$

54. $84 \div 7 \div 100 = \mathbf{0.12}$

55. $178 \div 4 \div 100 = \mathbf{0.445}$

56. $90 \div 3 \div 1,000 = \mathbf{0.03}$

57. $954 \div 6 \div 1,000 = \mathbf{0.159}$

58. $6.27 = \mathbf{62.7} \div 10 = \mathbf{627} \div 100$
$\quad = \mathbf{6,270} \div 1,000$

59. $179.4 = \mathbf{1,794} \div 10 = \mathbf{17,940} \div 100$
$\quad = \mathbf{179,400} \div 1,000$

60. $24.8 = 24,800 \div \mathbf{1,000} = 2,480 \div \mathbf{100}$
$\quad = 248 \div \mathbf{10}$

61. Press $\boxed{C}\boxed{2}\boxed{3}\boxed{.}\boxed{5}\boxed{5}\boxed{+}\boxed{1}\boxed{7}\boxed{.}\boxed{9}\boxed{5}\boxed{=}$
$41.50

62. Press $\boxed{C}\boxed{1}\boxed{0}\boxed{0}\boxed{.}\boxed{3}\boxed{-}\boxed{6}\boxed{2}\boxed{.}\boxed{0}\boxed{8}\boxed{=}$
38.22 cm

63. Press $\boxed{C}\boxed{4}\boxed{5}\boxed{.}\boxed{7}\boxed{\times}\boxed{9}\boxed{0}\boxed{=}$
4,113 yd.

64. Press C 5 3 . 9 1 5 ÷ 5 =
    10.783 kg

65. Press C 2 5 . 3 5 × 1 9 =
    $481.65

66. Press C 1 0 7 . 8 3 + 6 4 . 1 8 =
    172.01 gal.

67. Press C 3 5 4 9 . 2 0 − 9 3 7 . 9 5 =
    $2,611.25

68. Press C 2 . 8 6 4 × 4 7 =
    134.608 gal.

69. Press C 7 3 6 . 4 ÷ 3 5 =
    21.04 lb.

70. Press C 5 4 8 . 6 − 2 0 . 3 4 6 =
    528.254 L

71. $162.60 ÷ 12 = $13.55
    Each T-shirt costs **$13.55**.

72. $\frac{3}{4}$ × 1,000 = 750 g = 0.75 kg

    (12.45 × $30) + (0.75 × $18) = $387
    Mrs. Matthews spent **$387** altogether.

73. 79.15 − 16.75 = 62.4 lb.
    62.4 ÷ 10 = 6.24 lb.
    The mass of each metal ball is **6.24 lb**.

74. (a) $1 - \frac{1}{5} = \frac{4}{5}$

    $\frac{4}{5}$ × 17.3 = 13.84 m

    13.84 ÷ 4 = 3.46 m
    Joey used **3.46 m** of cloth to make 1 curtain.

    (b) 4 × $19.90 = $79.60
    He would receive **$79.60** altogether.

75.
8.6 lb.

| S | S | U | | | |

1.15   ?

5 units → 8.6 lb.
1 unit → 8.6 ÷ 5 = 1.72 lb.
3 units → 3 × 1.72 = 5.16 lb.
5.16 − 1.15 = 4.01 lb.
Her sister had **4.01 lb.** of sugar left.

76. 6 × $6.50 = $39
    3 × $4.65 = $13.95
    $39 + $13.95 = $52.95
    The least amount of money that Alex can pay is
    $52.95.

Unit 8: Conversion of Metric Measurements

1. 7.05 × 100 = **705 cm**
2. 9.163 × 100 = **916.3 cm**
3. 100.2 × 100 = **10,020 cm**
4. 1.755 × 1,000 = **1,755 m**
5. 24.82 × 1,000 = **24,820 m**
6. 69.95 × 1,000 = **69,950 m**
7. 5.105 × 1,000 = **5,105 g**
8. 30.4 × 1,000 = **30,400 g**
9. 171.7 × 1,000 = **171,700 g**

10. 0.126 × 1,000 = **126 mL**
11. 8.103 × 1,000 = **8,103 mL**
12. 19.6 × 1,000 = **19,600 mL**
13. 0.095 × 1,000 = 95 g
    70.095 kg = **70 kg 95 g**
14. 0.04 × 1000 = 40 mL
    66.04 L = **66 L 040 mL**
15. 0.96 × 100 = 96 cm
    13.96 m = **13 m 96 cm**
16. 0.5 × 100 = 50 cm
    45.5 m = **45 m 50 cm**
17. 0.137 × 1,000 = 137 mL
    4.137 L = **4 L 137 mL**
18. 0.016 × 1,000 = 16 m
    8.016 km = **8 km 16 m**
19. 0.4 × 100 = 40 cm
    312.4 m = **312 m 40 cm**
20. 0.58 × 1,000 = 580 g
    4.58 kg = **4 kg 580 g**
21. 439 ÷ 100 = **4.39 m**
22. 88.3 ÷ 100 = **0.883 m**
23. 969.5 ÷ 100 = **9.695 m**
24. 18 ÷ 1,000 = **0.018 km**
25. 616 ÷ 1,000 = **0.616 km**
26. 3,504 ÷ 1,000 = **3.504 km**
27. 97 ÷ 1,000 = **0.097 kg**
28. 402 ÷ 1,000 = **0.402 kg**
29. 3,610 ÷ 1,000 = **3.61 kg**
30. 25 ÷ 1,000 = **0.025 L**
31. 708 ÷ 1,000 = **0.708 L**
32. 60,900 ÷ 1,000 = **60.9 L**
33. 40 ÷ 100 = 0.4 m
    52 + 0.4 = **52.4 m**
34. 25 ÷ 1,000 = 0.025 km
    9 + 0.025 = **9.025 km**
35. 9 ÷ 1,000 = 0.009 kg
    8 + 0.009 = **8.009 kg**
36. 200 ÷ 1,000 = 0.2 L
    98 + 0.2 = **98.2 L**
37. 35 ÷ 1,000 = 0.035 kg
    37 + 0.035 = **37.035 kg**
38. 5 ÷ 1,000 = 0.005 L
    528 + 0.005 = **528.005 L**
39. 33 ÷ 100 = 0.33 m
    127 + 0.33 = **127.33 m**
40. 600 ÷ 1,000 = 0.6 km
    580 + 0.6 = **580.6 km**
41. 15 × 5 = 75 kg
    75 × 1,000 = 75,000 g
    The total mass of 15 bags of rice is **75,000 g**.
42. 36 ÷ 9 = 4
    4 × 5.5 = 22 L

$22 \times 1,000 = 22,000$ mL

The amount of water she uses to clean each bathroom is **22,000 mL**.

43. $2 \times 21.95 = 43.9$ km

$3 \times 43.9 = 131.7$ km

$131.7 \times 1,000 = 131,700$ m

The total distance he drives per day is **131,700 m**.

44. $6 \times 24 = 144$

$144 \times 390 = 56,160$ mL

$56,160 \div 1,000 = 56.16$ L

56.16 L of drinks are in the big container.

45. $195 \div 13 = 15$

$175 \times 15 = 2,625$ cm

$2,625 \div 100 = 26.25$ m

The length of ribbon that she uses to make 175 bookmarks is **26.25 m**.

46. (a) $255 \div 5 = 51$

$365 \times 51 = 18,615$

The chef makes **18,615** pizzas per year.

(b) $18,615 \times 175 = 3,257,625$ g

$3,257,625 \div 1,000 = 3,257.625$ kg

The chef needs **3,257.625 kg** of flour per year.

Review 1

1. **(1)**

$0.037 \times 1,000 = 37$ m

10.037 km $= 10$ km 37 m

2. **(1)**

$8 \div 1,000 = 0.008$

3. **(4)**

$18.25 = 18\frac{25}{100} = 18\frac{1}{4}$

4. **(2)**

$49.7 \div 100 = 0.497$ m

5. **(2)**

$25 \times 800 = 20,000$ g

$20,000 \div 1,000 = 20$ kg

6. **(1)**

$\$16.80 \div 14 = \$1.20$

7. **(1)**

$\$585 \div 6 = \$97.5$

$\$97.5 \div 10 = \$9.75$

8. **470.5 L**

$500 \div 1,000 = 0.5$ L

$470 + 0.5 = 470.5$ L

9. **$7,675.65**

Press C 7 8 8 5 . 6 0 − 2 0 9 . 9 5 =

10. **13,405 g**

$13.405 \times 1,000 = 13,405$ g

11. **3,540**

$7.08 \times 5 \times 100 = 35.4 \times 100$

$= 3,540$

12. **0.525 m**

$(22 - 4 - 4) \div 2 = 7$

$7 \times 7.5 = 52.5$ cm

$52.5 \div 100 = 0.525$ m

13. **0.197**

$197,000 \div 1,000 = 197$

$197 \div 100 = 1.97$

$1.97 \div 10 = 0.197$

14. **0.12**

$A \times 7 \times 10 = 8.4$

$A = 8.4 \div 7 \div 10$

$A = 0.12$

15. **40 people**

$\$19,260 \div \$481.50 = 40$

16. $24 \times 330 = 7,920$ mL

$7,920 \div 1,000 = 7.92$ L

The total capacity of the carton of mineral water was **7.92 L.**

17. $1,000 \times \$3.30 = \$3,300$

$80 \times \$4.20 = \$336$

$\$3,300 + \$336 = \$3,636$

Mr. Ali paid **$3,636** for all the lunches.

18. (a) $500 \div 20 = 25$

There are **25** packages of frozen chicken wings.

(b) $3 \times \$15.55 = \$46.65$

She will pay **$46.65**.

19. $12 \times 0.85 = 10.2$ L

$7 \times 0.75 = 5.25$ L

$10.2 - 5.25 = 4.95$ L $= 4,950$ mL

4,950 mL of milk are left after a week.

20. (a) $(8 \times 0.4) + (5 \times 0.4) = 5.2$ km

$5.2 \times 1,000 = 5,200$ m

The total distance both boys have run is **5,200 m.**

(b) $8 - 5 = 3$

$3 \times 0.4 = 1.2$ km

Zachary has run **1.2 km** farther than Cheng.

Unit 9: Averages

1. (a) $\$15 + \$18 + \$60 = $**$93**

(b) $\$93 \div 3 = $**$31**

2. (a) $268 + 208 + 109 = $**585 kg**

(b) $585 \div 3 = $**195 kg**

3. (a) $35 + 81 + 66 + 94 = $**276 in.**

(b) $276 \div 4 = $**69 in.**

4. (a) $358 + 92 + 189 + 93 = $**732 L**

(b) $732 \div 4 = $**183 L**

5. (a) $293 + 158 + 431 + 126 = $**1,008 in.**

(b) $1,008 \div 4 = $**252 in.**

6. $6 + 9 + 15 = 30$

$30 \div 3 = $**10**

7. $1 + 11 + 21 = 33$

$33 \div 3 = $**11**

8. $14 + 56 + 73 + 105 = 248$

$248 \div 4 = $**62**

9. $10 + 20 + 30 + 40 + 50 = 150$

$150 \div 5 = $**30**

10. $9 + 18 + 36 + 72 + 126 = 261$

$261 \div 5 = $**52.2**

11. $3.50 + $6.05 + $11 = $20.55
$20.55 ÷ 3 = **$6.85**

12. 0.75 + 1.4 + 3.36 + 9.6 + 21.09 = 36.2 kg
36.2 ÷ 5 = **7.24 kg**

13. 15.5 + 8.7 + 5.3 + 3.9 = 33.4 gal.
33.4 ÷ 4 = **8.35 gal.**

14. 48.7 + 99.3 + 132.5 = 280.5 km
280.5 ÷ 3 = **93.5 km**

15. 46 + 52 + 84 + 93 + 106 = 381 min.
381 ÷ 5 = **76.2 min.**

16. $200 + $180 + $280 + $300 + $265 = $1,225
$1,225 ÷ 5 = $245
The average amount of money Karim saved during this period of time was **$245**.

17. 146.5 × 4 = 586 cm
145 + 152 + 150 = 447 cm
586 − 447 = 139 cm
Daniel's height is **139 cm.**

18. (a) 72 + 85 + 70 + 79 = 306
The total points for the 4 subjects is **306**.
(b) 306 ÷ 4 = 76.5
The average points for the 4 subjects is **76.5**.

19. 369 × 5 = 1,845
1,845 − (608 + 411 + 227) = 599

599 − 569 = 30
30 ÷ 2 = 15
The number of bicycles that passed by the shop on that day was **15.**

20. 4 × 24.5 = 98
16 + 47 + 25 = 88
98 − 88 = 10
The last number is **10.**

21. 7 × 329 = 2,303
5 × 250 = 1,250
2,303 − 1,250 = 1,053
He sold **1,053** cans of drinks during the last 2 days.

22. 12.8 kg = 12,800 g
12,800 − 800 = 12,000 g
12,000 ÷ 160 = 75
There are **75** pens in the box.

23. 22 × 90 = 1,980¢ = $19.80
$27 + $19.80 = $46.80
$46.80 ÷ (22 + 18) = $1.17
The average lunch money of all the students in the class is **$1.17.**

24. (1 + 20) × 10 = 210
210 ÷ 20 = 10.5
The average of all the whole numbers ranging from 1 to 20 is **10.5.**

25. 8,450 − 5,250 = 3,200 g

3,200 ÷ 200 = 16
The number of red apples in the box is **16.**

26. (a) 10 × 47 = 470
470 − 326 = 144
453 − 144 = 309
The number of blue pens Uncle Ron had left was **309**.
(b) 309 + 471 = 780
780 ÷ 15 = 52
52 blue pens were in each box.

27. (a) 48 × 2 = 96
96 ÷ 4 = 24
3 × 24 = 72
Ella has **72** stickers.
(b) 41 × 2 = 82
82 − 24 = 58
Imani has **58** more stickers than Gina.

Unit 10: Percentages

1. $\frac{20}{100}$ = **0.2** $\frac{\overset{1}{\cancel{20}}}{\cancel{100}_{5}}$ = $\frac{1}{5}$

2. $\frac{45}{100}$ = **0.45** $\frac{\overset{9}{\cancel{45}}}{\cancel{100}_{20}}$ = $\frac{9}{20}$

3. $\frac{2}{100}$ = **0.02** $\frac{\overset{1}{\cancel{2}}}{\cancel{100}_{50}}$ = $\frac{1}{50}$

4. $\frac{89}{100}$ = **0.89** $\frac{89}{100}$ = $\frac{89}{100}$

5. $\frac{72}{100}$ = **0.72** $\frac{\overset{18}{\cancel{72}}}{\cancel{100}_{25}}$ = $\frac{18}{25}$

6. 0.3 = 0.30 = $\frac{30}{100}$ = **30%**

7. 0.05 = $\frac{5}{100}$ = **5%**

8. 0.64 = $\frac{64}{100}$ = **64%**

9. 0.17 = $\frac{17}{100}$ = **17%**

10. 0.94 = $\frac{94}{100}$ = **94%**

11. 0.42 = $\frac{42}{100}$ = **42%**

12. 0.58 = $\frac{58}{100}$ = **58%**

13. 0.23 = $\frac{23}{100}$ = **23%**

14. 0.76 = $\frac{76}{100}$ = **76%**

15. 0.8 = 0.80 = $\frac{80}{100}$ = **80%**

16. $\frac{1}{2}$ = $\frac{50}{100}$ = **50%**

17. $\frac{9}{10}$ = $\frac{90}{100}$ = **90%**

18. $\frac{16}{25}$ = $\frac{64}{100}$ = **64%**

19. $\dfrac{18}{200} = \dfrac{9}{100} =$ **9%**

20. $\dfrac{240}{400} = \dfrac{60}{100} =$ **60%**

21. $\dfrac{3}{4} = \dfrac{75}{100} =$ **75%**

22. $\dfrac{2}{5} = \dfrac{40}{100} =$ **40%**

23. $\dfrac{11}{20} = \dfrac{55}{100} =$ **55%**

24. $\dfrac{59}{100} =$ **59%**

25. $\dfrac{350}{500} = \dfrac{70}{100} =$ **70%**

26. $\dfrac{20}{100} \times 150 =$ **30**

27. $\dfrac{16}{100} \times 800 =$ **$128**

28. $\dfrac{80}{100} \times 55 =$ **44 kg**

29. $\dfrac{35}{100} \times 220 =$ **77 mi.**

30. $\dfrac{40}{100} \times 3,300 =$ **$1,320**

31. $\dfrac{88}{100} \times 250 =$ **220**

32. $\dfrac{64}{100} \times 450 =$ **288**

33. $\dfrac{9}{100} \times 1,000 =$ **$90**

34. $\dfrac{75}{100} \times 600 =$ **450 m**

35. $\dfrac{50}{100} \times 32 =$ **16 lb.**

36. **57%**

   $100 - 43 = 57$

   $\dfrac{57}{100} = 57\%$

37. **80%**

   $\dfrac{8}{10} = \dfrac{80}{100} = 80\%$

38. **75%**

   $1 - \dfrac{1}{4} = \dfrac{3}{4}$

   $\dfrac{3}{4} \times 100 = 75\%$

39. **50%**

   $\dfrac{1}{2} \times 300 = 150$

   $\dfrac{150}{300} \times 100 = 50\%$

40. **40%**

   $600 - 360 = 240$

   $\dfrac{240}{600} \times 100 = 40\%$

41. **$180**

   $\dfrac{15}{100} \times 1,200 = \$180$

42. **26 students**

   $100 - 35 = 65\%$

   $\dfrac{65}{100} \times 40 = 26$

43. **960 computers**

   $\dfrac{20}{100} \times 800 = 160$

   $800 + 160 = 960$

44. **$1,960**

   $100\% - 20\% = 80\%$

   $\dfrac{80}{100} \times 2,450 = \$1,960$

45. **$180**

   $\dfrac{4.5}{100} \times 4,000 = \$180$

46. $\dfrac{20}{100} \times 900 = \$180$

   $\$900 - \$180 = \$720$

   Jiang paid **$720** for the bicycle.

47. (a) $100 - 35 - 25 = 40\%$

   Charlie received **40%** of the beads.

   (b) $40\% \rightarrow 600$

   $1\% \rightarrow 600 \div 40 = 15$

   $35\% \rightarrow 35 \times 15 = 525$

   Amira received **525** beads.

48. $100 - 45 - 20 = 35\%$

   $\dfrac{35}{100} \times 80 = 28$

   The store owner had **28 kg** of rice left.

49. $\dfrac{7}{100} \times 375 = \$26.25$

   $\$375 + \$26.25 = \$401.25$

   The total cost of the hotel rooms was **$401.25**.

50. (a) $100 - 40 = 60\%$

   $60\% \rightarrow 48$

   $10\% \rightarrow 8$

   $100\% \rightarrow 10 \times 8 = 80$

   There are **80** blue pens.

   (b) $100 - 25 - 35 = 40\%$

   $40\% \rightarrow 80$

   $10\% \rightarrow 80 \div 4 = 20$

   $100\% \rightarrow 10 \times 20 = 200$

   There are **200** pens altogether in the box.

51. (a) $100 - 60 = 40\%$

   $60 - 40 = 20\%$

   There are **20%** more chicken eggs than duck eggs.

   (b) $20\% \rightarrow 420$

   $40\% \rightarrow 2 \times 420 = 840$

   The farmer has **840** duck eggs.

   (c) $840 + 420 = 1,260$

   $(1,260 \times 15¢) + (840 \times 23¢) = 38,220¢$
   $\qquad\qquad\qquad\qquad\qquad\quad = \$382.20$

   The farmer makes **$382.20**.

52. (a) $\dfrac{15}{100} \times 890 = \$133.50$

   $\$890 - \$133.50 = \$756.50$

   The laptop computer was **$756.50** after the discount.

   (b) $\$756.50 \div 5 = \$151.30$

   She would have to pay **$151.30** each month.

53. (a) $\dfrac{45}{100} \times 250,000 = \$112,500$

   His wife received **$112,500**.

117

(b) $\dfrac{33}{100} \times 250{,}0\cancel{0}\cancel{0} = \$82{,}500$

    His son received **$82,500**.

(c) $\$250{,}000 - \$112{,}500 - \$82{,}500 = \$55{,}000$

    $\$55{,}000 \div 2 = \$27{,}500$

    Each of his daughters received **$27,500**.

Review 2

1. **(3)**
 $\dfrac{64}{400} = \dfrac{16}{100} = 16\%$

2. **(2)**
 $\$815 \div 5 = \$163$

3. **(1)**
 $0.03 = \dfrac{3}{100} = 3\%$

4. **(3)**
 $32 \times 72 = 2{,}304$

5. **(3)**
 $100 - 10 = 90\%$
 $90\% \rightarrow 180$
 $10\% \rightarrow 180 \div 9 = 20$
 $100\% \rightarrow 20 \times 10 = 200$

6. **(2)**
 $\left(\dfrac{7}{100} \times \$20\right) + \left(\dfrac{60}{100} \times \$3\right) = \$3.20$

7. **(4)**
 $\dfrac{20}{100} \times 3 = \dfrac{3}{5}$ yd. $\dfrac{10}{100} \times 6 = \dfrac{3}{5}$ yd.
 $\dfrac{5}{100} \times 12 = \dfrac{3}{5}$ yd. $\dfrac{25}{100} \times 2 = \dfrac{1}{2}$ yd.

8. **$\dfrac{12}{25}$**
 $\dfrac{48}{100} = \dfrac{12}{25}$

9. **20%**
 $192 + 48 = 240$
 $\dfrac{48}{240} \times 100 = 20\%$

10. **52 in.**
 $8 + 48 = 56$ in.
 $48 + 56 = 104$ in.
 $104 \div 2 = 52$ in.

11. **1.64 m**
 $(6 \times 1.6) - (4 \times 1.58) = 3.28$ m
 $3.28 \div 2 = 1.64$ m

12. **60%**
 $1 - \dfrac{2}{5} = \dfrac{3}{5}$ $\dfrac{3}{\cancel{5}_1} \times \cancel{100}^{20} = 60\%$

13. **$346.50**
 $\left(\dfrac{20}{100} \times 315\right) + 315 = \$378$
 $(\$315 + \$378) \div 2 = \$346.50$

14. **1,400 g**
 $100 - 65 = 35\%$
 $\dfrac{35}{100} \times 4{,}000 = 1{,}400$ g

15. **31.7**
 $6 \times 8.9 = 53.4$
 $6.5 + 3.8 + 4.1 + 7.3 = 21.7$
 $53.4 - 21.7 = 31.7$

16. (a) $(63 + 74) \div 2 = 68.5$
     $68.5 - 4 = 64.5$
     The average number of points Maggie received on her Math and Science tests was **64.5**.

 (b) $64.5 \times 2 = 129$
     $129 - 55 = 74$
     Maggie got **74** points on her Math test.

17.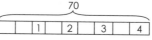
 $5 \text{ parts} + 1 + 2 + 3 + 4 = 5 \times 14$
     $5 \text{ parts} + 10 = 70$
         $5 \text{ parts} = 70 - 10$
             $1 \text{ part} = 60 \div 5 = 12$
 $12 + 13 + 14 + 15 + 16 = 70$
 The five numbers are **12**, **13**, **14**, **15**, and **16**.

18. (a) $\dfrac{35}{100} \times 4{,}600 = 1{,}610$
     $4{,}600 - 1{,}610 - 920 = 2{,}070$
     The factory produces **2,070** dresses.

 (b) $\dfrac{2{,}070}{4{,}600} \times 10\cancel{0} = 45$
     45% of the pieces of clothing are dresses.

19. (a) $120\% \rightarrow \$10.20$
     $1\% \rightarrow 10.20 \div 120 = \$0.085$
     $100\% \rightarrow 100 \times 0.085 = \$8.50$
     His normal hourly wage is **$8.50**.

 (b) $(\$8.50 \times 8) + \$10.20 = \$78.20$
     He earns **$78.20** on that day.

20. $\dfrac{3}{100} \times 1{,}200 = \$36$
 $\$1{,}200 + \$36 = \$1{,}236$
 Jamila will have **$1,236** in her savings account at the end of this year.

Unit 11: Angles

1. $\angle u = \mathbf{100°}$
 $\angle t + \angle u = 80° + 100° = \mathbf{180°}$

2. $\angle y = \mathbf{245°}$
 $\angle x + \angle y = 115° + 245° = \mathbf{360°}$

3. $\angle b = \mathbf{42°}$
 $\angle a + \angle b = 318° + 42° = \mathbf{360°}$

4. (a) $\angle a = \mathbf{75°}$
     $\angle b = \mathbf{105°}$
     $\angle c = \mathbf{75°}$
     $\angle d = \mathbf{105°}$

 (b) **vertically opposite**
 (c) **vertically opposite**
 (d) **angles on a straight line**
 (e) **angles at a point**

5. (a) **180°** (angles on a straight line)
 (b) $\angle \mathbf{a}$, $\angle \mathbf{b}$, and $\angle \mathbf{c}$ or $\angle \mathbf{d}$ and $\angle \mathbf{e}$
 (c) $\angle \mathbf{b}$ and $\angle \mathbf{c}$
 (d) $360° - 90° = \mathbf{270°}$ (angles at a point)

6. $\angle AOC = 180° - 28° = \mathbf{152°}$
 (angles on a straight line)

∠DOB = ∠AOC = **152°**
(vertically opposite angles)
∠COB = ∠AOD = **28°**
(vertically opposite angles)

7. ∠WOY = 180° − 118° − 25° = **37°**
(angles on a straight line)

8. ∠DOE = 180° − 77° − 45° − 18° = **40°**
(angles on a straight line)

9. ∠SOV = 180° − 90° − 69° = **21°**
(angles on a straight line)

10. ∠AOB = 360° − 96° = **264°**
(angles at a point)

11. ∠a = 360° − 122° − 58° − 101° = **79°**
(angles at a point)

12. ∠e = 360° − 194° − 90° = **76°**
(angles at a point)

13. ∠x = 360° − 112° − 87° − 93°
    = **68°** (angles at a point)

14. ∠y = (180° − 90°) ÷ 2
    = **45°** (angles on a straight line)

15. ∠b + ∠4b = 360° − 90° − 90° (angles at a point)
    ∠5b = 180°
    ∠b = 180° ÷ 5 = **36°**
    ∠4b = 4 × 36° = **144°**

16. ∠m = 180° − 125° − 45°
    = **10°** (angles on a straight line)

17. ∠2p + ∠p = 360° − 200° − 88°
    ∠3p = 72° (angles at a point)
    ∠p = 72° ÷ 3 = **24°**
    ∠2p = 2 × 24° = **48°**

Unit 12: Triangles and 4-Sided Figures

1. ∠ABC = 180° − 58° − 63°
    = **59°** (sum of ∠s in a triangle = 180°)

2. ∠YXZ = 180° − 90° − 49°
    = **41°** (sum of ∠s in a triangle = 180°)

3. ∠NLM = 180° − 116° − 25°
    = **39°** (sum of ∠s in a triangle = 180°)

4. ∠ACB = (180° − 42°) ÷ 2
    = **69°** (isosceles triangle)

5. ∠EHF = ∠EFH = 180° − 59° − 53°
    = **68°** (isosceles triangle)

6. ∠RPQ = ∠PRQ = 60° (equilateral triangle)
    ∠RPS = 60° − 24° = 36°
    ∠PSR = 180° − 36° − 60°
    = **84°** (sum of ∠s in a triangle = 180°)

7. ∠DCB = ∠DBC = 31° (isosceles triangle)
    ∠CDB = 180° − 31° − 31°
    = 118° (sum of ∠s in a triangle = 180°)
    ∠ADC = 180° − 118°
    = **62°** (angles on a straight line)

8. ∠PRQ = 60° (equilateral triangle)
    ∠PRS = 124° − 60° = 64°

∠SPR = 180° − 90° − 64°
    = **26°** (sum of ∠s in a triangle = 180°)

9. ∠ABC = (180° − 124°) ÷ 2
    = 28° (isosceles triangle)
    ∠EBD = 180° − 90° − 59°
    = 31° (sum of ∠s in a triangle = 180°)
    ∠ABD = 28° + 31° = **59°**

10. ∠a = 180° − 110° − 35°
    = **35°** (sum of ∠s in a triangle = 180°)
    It is an **isosceles** triangle.

11. ∠b = 180° − 60° − 60°
    = **60°** (sum of ∠s in a triangle = 180°)
    It is an **equilateral** triangle.

12. ∠c = 180° − 70° − 30°
    = **80°** (sum of ∠s in a triangle = 180°)

13. ∠d = 180° − 25° − 65°
    = **90°** (sum of ∠s in a triangle = 180°)
    It is a **right-angled** triangle.

14. ∠e = 180° − 65° − 50°
    = **65°** (sum of ∠s in a triangle = 180°)
    It is an **isosceles** triangle.

15. ∠f = 180° − 130° − 15°
    = **35°** (sum of ∠s in a triangle = 180°)

16. ∠a = **110°** (opp. ∠s of a parallelogram are equal)

17. ∠b = 180° − 60°
    = **120°** (∠s between parallel sides add up to 180°)

18. ∠WZY = ∠WXY = 70° (opp. ∠s of a parallelogram are equal)
    ∠c = 180° − 70° − 70°
    = **40°** (sum of ∠s in a triangle = 180°)

19. ∠d = **135°** (opp. ∠s of a parallelogram are equal)

20. ∠e = 180° − 123°
    = **57°** (∠s between parallel sides add up to 180°)
    ∠f = 180° − 98°
    = **82°** (∠s between parallel sides add up to 180°)

21. ∠PSR = 180° − 38°
    = 142° (∠s between parallel sides add up to 180°)
    ∠g = 142° − 40° = **102°**

22. ∠TRU = (180° − 70°) ÷ 2
    = 55° (sum of ∠s in a triangle = 180°)
    ∠SRU = 180° − 90°
    = 90° (∠s between parallel sides add up to 180°)
    ∠h = 90° − 55° = **35°**

23. ∠BAC = 35° (isosceles triangle)
    ∠i = 180° − 35° − 35°
    = **110°** (sum of ∠s in a triangle = 180°)

24. ∠j = 180° − 105°
    = **75°** (∠s between parallel sides add up to 180°)

25. ∠JNM = 180° ÷ 3
    = 60° (equilateral triangle)
    ∠JNL = 180° − 60°
    = 120° (∠s on a straight line)
    ∠k = **120°** (opp. ∠s of a rhombus are equal)

26. ∠PSR = 180° − 82°
    = **98°** (∠s between parallel sides add up to 180°)

27. ∠BAD = ∠DCB
    = 118° (opp. ∠s of a parallelogram are equal)
    ∠ACD = 118° − 68° = **50°**

28. ∠WXZ = 180° − 90° − 61°
    = **29°** (sum of ∠s in a triangle = 180°)
    ∠WZY = ∠WXY = 90° + 29° = 119°
    (opp. ∠s of a parallelogram are equal)
    ∠XZY = 119° − 90° = **29°**
    ∠XYZ = 180° − 90° − 29°
    = **61°** (sum of ∠s in a triangle = 180°)

29. ∠CAD = 180° − 68° − 57°
    = **55°** (∠s between parallel sides add up to 180°)

30. ∠PQR = ∠POR
    = 70° (opp. ∠s of a parallelogram are equal)
    ∠PQS = 70° − 32° = **38°**
    ∠ORQ = 180° − 70°
    = 110° (∠s between parallel sides add up to 180°)
    ∠ORP = 180° − 47° − 70°
    = 63° (sum of ∠s in a triangle = 180°)
    ∠QRS = 110° − 63° = **47°**

31. ∠ZWX = ∠ZYX
    = 115° (opp. ∠s of a parallelogram are equal)
    ∠YWX = 115° − 70° = **45°**
    ∠ZXY = 180° − 115° − 30°
    = 35° (sum of ∠s in a triangle = 180°)
    ∠WXY = 180° − 115°
    = 65° (∠s between parallel sides add up to 180°)
    ∠WXZ = 65° − 35° = **30°**

Review 3

1. **(3)**
   A rhombus has 4 equal sides and parallel opposite sides.

2. **(4)**
   180° − 112° − 34° = 34°
   In an isosceles triangle, angles opposite the equal sides are equal.

3. **(1)**
   ∠BAC = ∠ACB = 62° (isosceles triangle)
   ∠ABC = 180° − 62° − 62°
   = 56° (sum of ∠s in a triangle = 180°)

4. **(1)**
   ∠XWZ = ∠WZX = ∠ZXW = 60° (equilateral triangle)
   ∠XZY = 180° − 60° = 120° (∠s on a straight line)
   ∠ZXY = 180° − 35° − 120°
   = 25° (sum of ∠s in a triangle = 180°)

5. **(2)**
   ∠d = 180° − 133°
   = 47° (∠s between parallel sides add up to 180°)

6. **(3)**
   ∠p = 180° − 35° = 145° (∠s on a straight line)

7. **(4)**
   ∠q = 180° − 90° − 35° = 55° (∠s on a straight line)
   ∠p + ∠q = 145° + 55° = 200°

8. **71°**
   ∠EAD = ∠AED = ∠EDA = 60° (equilateral triangle)
   ∠ECD = ∠DEC = (180° − 120°) ÷ 2
   = 30° (isosceles triangle)
   ∠EBC = 180° − 60° − 30° − 19°
   = 71° (sum of ∠s in a triangle = 180°)

9. **180°**
   ∠SRQ = ∠SPQ = 137° (opp. ∠s are equal)
   ∠PQR = 180° − 137°
   = 43° (∠s between parallel sides add up to 180°)
   ∠SRQ + ∠PQR = 137° + 43° = 180°

10. **6°**
    ∠CED = ∠DCE = 58° (isosceles triangle)
    ∠DEF = 180° − 116° = 64°
    ∠CEF = 64° − 58° = 6°

11. **360°**
    180° × 2 = 360° (∠s in an equilateral triangle = 180°)

12. **104°**
    ∠SPQ = ∠QRS = 104° (opp. ∠s are equal)

13. **105°**
    ∠EOF = 60°
    ∠AOB = 45°
    ∠EOF + ∠AOB = 60° + 45° = 105°

14. ∠VWX = 180° − 79°
    = **101°** (∠s between parallel sides add up to 180°)
    ∠TUV = 180° − 71°
    = 109° (∠s between parallel sides add up to 180°)
    ∠VUX = 180° − 109° = **71°** (∠s on a straight line)

15. **160°**
    4b + 3b + 2b = 360° (∠s at a point)
    9b = 360°
    b = 360° ÷ 9 = 40°
    4b = 4 × 40° = 160°

16. **115°**
    ∠a = 180° − 18° − 57° − 33°
    = 72° (∠s on a straight line)
    ∠c = 180° − 57° − 33° − 47°
    = 43° (∠s on a straight line)
    ∠a + ∠c = 72° + 43° = 115°

17. **108°**
    ∠ADB = (180° − 84°) ÷ 2
    = 48° (isosceles triangle)
    ∠BAC = 60° (equilateral triangle)
    ∠EAD = 84° − 60° = 24°
    ∠x = 180° − 48° − 24°
    = 108° (sum of ∠s in a triangle = 180°)

18. **78°**
    ∠PTS = ∠SPT = ∠TSP = 60° (equilateral triangle)
    ∠PQR = 180° − 72°
    = 108°
    (∠s between the parallel sides add up to 180°)
    ∠TPQ = 180° − 60°
    = 120°
    (∠s between the parallel sides add up to 180°)
    ∠PQT = ∠PTQ = (180° − 120°) ÷ 2 = 30°

$\angle a = 108° - 30° = 78°$

19. **120°**

$$4a + a + a = 180° \text{ (sum of } \angle s \text{ in a triangle} = 180°)$$
$$6a = 180°$$
$$a = 180° \div 6 = 30°$$
$$4a = 4 \times 30° = 120°$$

20. **69°**

$$\angle CBE = \angle CEB = (180° - 42°) \div 2$$
$$= 69° \text{ (isosceles triangle)}$$
$$\angle ABC = 180° - 69° = 111° (\angle s \text{ on a straight line})$$
$$\angle BCD = 180° - 111°$$
$$= 69° (\angle s \text{ between parallel sides add up to } 180°)$$

Unit 13: Geometrical Construction

1. ***(See Diagram 1 on page 127)***

   Step 1: Draw Line AB 6 cm long using a ruler.

   Step 2: Measure and draw an angle of 80° at Point A using a protractor.

   Step 3: Measure and draw an angle of 45° at Point B using the protractor. Join Points B and C by drawing a line using the ruler.

2. ***(See Diagram 2 on page 127)***

   Step 1: Draw Line FG 7 cm long using a ruler.

   Step 2: Place a set square on Line FG, making sure a right angle is formed.

   Step 3: Draw Line FE 4 cm long with the set square and ruler.

   Step 4: Join Points E and G by drawing a line using the ruler.

3. ***(See Diagram 3 on page 127)***

   Step 1: Draw Line AB 5 cm long using a ruler.

   Step 2: Draw an angle of 60° at Point B using a protractor.

   Step 3: Extend the line drawn from Point B to 3 cm using the ruler.

   Step 4: Draw Line CD 5 cm long using the ruler and set square. Make sure Line CD is parallel to Line AB.

   Step 5: Join Points D and A by drawing a line using the ruler.

4. ***(See Diagram 4 on page 127)***

   Step 1: Draw Line OP 4.5 cm long using a ruler.

   Step 2: Draw a line 4.5 cm long at Point O with a set square and ruler. Make sure this line is perpendicular to Line OP. Do the same at Point P. Label the 2 points as R and Q respectively.

   Step 3: Join Points R and Q by drawing a line using the ruler.

5. ***(See Diagram 5 on page 127)***

   Step 1: Draw Line WX 5 cm long using a ruler.

   Step 2: Draw a line 3 cm long at Point W with a set square and ruler. Make sure this line is perpendicular to Line WX. Do the same at Point X. Label the 2 points as Z and Y respectively.

   Step 3: Join Points Z and Y by drawing a line using the ruler.

6. ***(See Diagram 6 on page 127)***

   Step 1: Draw Line FG 3.5 cm long using a ruler.

   Step 2: Draw an angle of 70° at Point F using a protractor.

   Step 3: Extend the line drawn from Point F to 3.5 cm using the ruler. Label the line as FE.

   Step 4: Draw Line EH 3.5 cm long using the ruler and set square. Make sure EH is parallel to FG.

   Step 5: Join Points H and G by drawing a line using the ruler.

7. ***(See Diagram 7 on page 127)***

   Step 1: Draw Line EF 7 cm long using a ruler.

   Step 2: Draw an angle of 50° at Point E using a protractor.

   Step 3: Extend the line drawn from Point E to 6 cm using the ruler. Label the line as EC.

   Step 4: Draw Line CD using the ruler and set square. Make sure CD is parallel to EF.

   Step 5: Draw an angle of 75° at Point F using a protractor. Join Points F and D by drawing a line using the ruler.

Unit 14: Volume

1. **7**
2. **10**
3. **9**
4.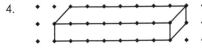
5.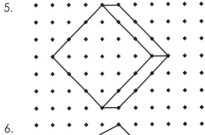
6.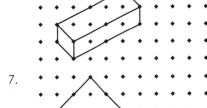
7.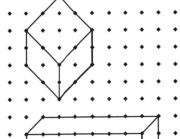
8.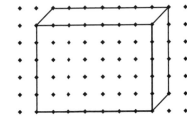

121

Singapore Math Practice Level 5B

9. **10 cm³**
   Volume of each cube = 1 × 1 × 1 = 1 cm³
   Volume of the solid = 10 × 1 = 10 cm³

10. **13 cm³**
    Volume = 13 × 1 = 13 cm³

11. **18 cm³**
    Volume = 18 × 1 = 18 cm³

12. Length = **4 cm**
    Width = **3 cm**
    Height = **6 cm**
    Volume = 4 × 3 × 6 = **72 cm³**

13. Length = **5 cm**
    Width = **5 cm**
    Height = **5 cm**
    Volume = 5 × 5 × 5 = **125 cm³**

14. Length = **25 cm**
    Width = **3 cm**
    Height = **3 cm**
    Volume = 25 × 3 × 3 = **225 cm³**

15. Length = **16 cm**
    Width = **7 cm**
    Height = **9 cm**
    Volume = 16 × 7 × 9 = **1,008 cm³**

16. Edge = **9 in.**
    Volume = 9 × 9 × 9 = **729 in.³**

17. Edge = **11 cm**
    Volume = 11 × 11 × 11 = **1,331 cm³**

18. **960 in.³**
    Volume = 10 × 8 × 12 = 960

19. **360 cm³**
    Volume = 4 × 5 × 18 = 360

20. **3,375 ft.³**
    Volume = 15 × 15 × 15 = 3,375

21. **81 cm³**
    Volume = 3 × 3 × 9 = 81

22. **17,576 in.³**
    Volume = 26 × 26 × 26 = 17,576

23. **315 cm³**
    315 mL = 315 cm³

24. **1,200 cm³**
    1 L = 1,000 mL = 1,000 cm³
    1 L 200 mL = 1,000 + 200 = 1,200 cm³

25. **19,003 cm³**
    19 L = 19,000 mL = 19,000 cm³
    19 L 3 mL = 19,000 + 3 = 19,003 cm³

26. **59 cm³**
    59 mL = 59 cm³

27. **43,007 cm³**
    43 L = 43,000 mL = 43,000 cm³
    43 L 7 mL = 43,000 + 7 = 43,007 cm³

28. **20,088 cm³**
    20 L = 20,000 mL = 20,000 cm³

20 L 88 mL = 20,000 + 88
            = 20,088 cm³

29. **755 mL**
    755 cm³ = 755 mL

30. **3 L 4 mL**
    3,004 cm² = 3,000 mL + 4 mL
              = 3 L 4 mL

31. **5 L 60 mL**
    5,060 cm³ = 5,000 mL + 60 mL
              = 5 L 60 mL

32. **75 L 70 mL**
    75,070 cm³ = 75,000 mL + 70 mL
               = 75 L 70 mL

33. **14 L 5 mL**
    14,005 cm³ = 14,000 mL + 5 mL
               = 14 L 5 mL

34. **48 L 276 mL**
    48,276 cm³ = 48,000 mL + 276 mL
               = 48 L 276 mL

35. 13 × 25 × 12 = 3,900 in.³
    Its capacity is **3,900 in.³**.

36. 13 × 13 × 13 = 2,197 cm³ ÷ 100
                 = 21.97 m³
    Its volume is **21.97 m³**.

37. 38 × 17 × 9.5 = 6,137 in.³
    Its volume is **6,137 in.³**.

38. $\frac{1}{2}$ × 600 × 19 = 5,700 cm³ ÷ 1,000
                 = 5.7 L
    5.7 L of water are needed to fill the tank completely.

39. 24 × 24 × 24 = 13,824 cm³
    13,824 ÷ 384 = 36
    He will need **36** bottles of water to fill the tank completely.

40. (a) $1 - \frac{3}{4} = \frac{1}{4}$
        $\frac{1}{4}$ × 30 × 12.5 × 20 = 1,875 cm³ ÷ 1,000
                         = 1.875 L
        1.875 L of water are needed to fill the tank to its brim.

    (b) 1,875 ÷ 3 = 625
        625 cm³ of water flows from the tap per minute.

41. 70 × 90 × 110 = 693,000 in.³
    693,000 − 5,880 = 687,120 in.³
    687,120 in.³ of water are in the fish pond.

42. 100 − 75 = 25 %
    $\frac{25}{100}$ × 48 × 38 × 28 = 12,768 cm³
    12,768 cm³ of water will be needed to completely fill the tank.

43. 1.5 L = 1.5 × 1,000 = 1,500 cm³
    5 × 5 × 6 = 150 cm³
    1,500 ÷ 150 = 10
    10 beakers of water are needed to fill the bucket.

44. (a) $\frac{2}{3}$ × 18 × 26 × 24 = 7,488

The volume of water in the tank is **7,488 in.³**.

(b) 13 × 16 × 9 = 1,872 in.³
7,488 + 1,872 = 9,360
The new volume of water in the tank is **9,360 in.³**.

45. $\frac{3}{4}$ × 40 × 40 × 41.25 = 49,500 cm³
4.5 L = 4.5 × 1,000 = 4,500 mL
= 4,500 cm³
49,500 ÷ 4,500 = 11
Ethan should let the water run for **11 minutes** if he wants to fill $\frac{3}{4}$ of the tank.

Review 4

1. **(4)**
4 L = 4 × 1,000 = 4,000 cm³
4 L 325 mL = 4,000 + 325 = 4,325 cm³

2. **(2)**
Base area = 8 × 8 = 64 in.²
Volume = 8 × 8 × 8 = 512 in.³

3. **(3)**

4. **(4)**
24 × 13 × 7 = 2,184 in.³

5. **(2)**
10,040 = 10,000 + 40 = 10 L 40 mL

6. **(4)**
ABCD is a trapezoid with one pair of parallel opposite sides.

7. **(1)**
$1 - \frac{3}{4} = \frac{1}{4}$
$\frac{1}{4}$ × 18 × 12 × 10 = 540 in.³

8. **(2)**
70 × 70 × 70 = 343,000 cm³
7 L = 7,000 cm³
343,000 ÷ 7,000 = 49

9. **120°**
Use a protractor to measure ∠ABC.

10. **80 in.³**
Volume = 5 × 4 × 4 = 80 in.³

11. **12,012 cm³**
1,000 mL = 1,000 cm³
12,012 mL = 12,012 cm³

12. **3,168 in.³**
16 × 18 × 11 = 3,168 in.³

13. **trapezoid**
This figure has a pair of parallel opposite sides, so it must be a trapezoid.

14. **rhombus**

15. **11 cups**
Volume = $\frac{1}{4}$ × 121 × 8 = 242 cm³
242 ÷ 22 = 11

16. **1 in.**
Volume = 5 × 6 × H

30 in.³ = 30 × H
H = 30 ÷ 30 = 1 in.

17. **(See Diagram 8 on page 127)**
Step 1: Draw Line EF 3.5 cm long using a ruler.
Step 2: Draw a line 3.5 cm long at Point E with a set square and ruler. Make sure this line is perpendicular to Line EF. Do the same at Point F. Label the 2 points as H and G respectively.
Step 3: Join Points H and G by drawing a line using the ruler.

18. $\frac{1}{5}$ × 45 × 24 × 30 = 6,480 in.³

She takes **6,480 in.³** of water.

19. **(See Diagram 9 on page 127)**
Step 1: Draw Line WX 4 cm long using a ruler.
Step 2: Draw an angle of 50° at Point W using c protractor.
Step 3: Extend the line drawn from Point W to 3 cr using the ruler.
Step 4: Draw Line ZY 4 cm long using the ruler and s square. Make sure Line ZY is parallel to Li WX.
Step 5: Join Points Y and X by drawing a line using ruler and set square.

20. Volume = $\frac{1}{2}$ × 896 × 22 = 9,856 cm³
9,856 ÷ 44 = 224
The cup must be used **224 times** to empty the w er from the container.

Final Review

1. **(2)**
550 × 30 min. = 16,500 cm³
16,500 ÷ 1,000 = 16.5 L

2. **(1)**
180° − 90° − 63° = 27° (∠s on a straight line)

3. **(2)**
∠BCD = 180° − 52°
= 128° (∠s between parallel sides add (180°)
∠x = 180° − 128°
= 52° (∠s on a straight line)

4. **(1)**
Each pair of angles between the *paralle* es of a rhombus adds up to 180°.

5. **(3)**
8 − 6 = 2 in.
13 × 10 × 6 = 780 in.³

6. **(2)**
∠ACB = 180° − 125° = 55° (∠s on a straig e)
∠ABC = 180° − 20° − 55°
= 105° (sum of ∠s in a triangle =)
∠CBD = 180° − 105°
= 75° (∠s on a straight line)

7. **(1)**
0.052 × 1,000 = 52 mL
8.052 L = 8,000 mL + 52 mL
= 8 L 52 mL

Singapore Math Practice Level 5B

8. **(2)**
$\angle a = 180° - 128°$
$= 52°$ ($\angle$s on a straight line)
$\angle c = 180° - 35° - 52° - 52°$
$= 41°$ ($\angle$s on straight line)
$\angle a + \angle c = 52° + 41° = 93°$

9. **(2)**
$100\% + 7\% \rightarrow \$561.75$
$107\% \rightarrow \$561.75$
$1\% \rightarrow \$561.75 \div 107 = \$5.25$
$100\% \rightarrow \$5.25 \times 100 = \$525$

10. **(4)**
$180° - 50° - 63° = 67°$ (sum of $\angle$s in a triangle = 180°)

11. **(4)**
Average height of a girl = $327 \div 3 = 109$ cm
Total height of 2 boys = $535 - 327 = 208$ cm
Average height of a boy = $208 \div 2 = 104$ cm
$109 - 104 = 5$ cm

12. **(2)**
$100\% - 45\% - 15\% = 40\%$
$\frac{40}{100} \times 72 = 28.8$ kg
$28.8 \times 1,000 = 28,800$ g

13. **(2)**
$97.8 = 0.978 \times 100$

14. **(3)**
$\angle ABD = 180° - 90° - 24°$
$= 66°$ (sum of $\angle$s in a triangle = 180°)
$\angle ABC = 180° - 66°$
$= 114°$ ($\angle$s on a straight line)

15. **(3)**
Figure (3) has 2 pairs of parallel opposite sides. It is a parallelogram.

16. **0.104**
$104 \div 1,000 = 0.104$

17. **$38.87**
$13 \times \$2.99 = \$38.87$

18. **2%**
$0.02 = \frac{2}{100} = 2\%$

19. **109 kg**
$42 \times 3 = 126$ kg

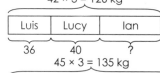

$45 \times 3 = 135$ kg

$3 \times 42 = 126$ kg
$126 - 36 - 40 = 50$ kg
$3 \times 45 = 135$ kg
$135 - 36 - 40 = 59$ kg
$50 + 59 = 109$ kg

20. **$32.40**
$\frac{54}{100} \times \$60 = \$32.40$

21. **25,200 mL**
$1.8 \times 7 \times 2 = 25.2$ L
$25.2 \times 1,000 = 25,200$ mL

22. **50°, right-angled triangle**
$\angle OQP = 180° - 90° - 40°$
$= 50°$ (sum of $\angle$s in a triangle = 180°)
OPQ is a right-angled triangle.

23. **62°**
$\angle TUS = 180° - 144°$
$= 36°$ ($\angle$s on a straight line)
$\angle STU = 180° - 82° - 36°$
$= 62°$ (sum of $\angle$s in a triangle = 180°)

24. **28 gal.**
$100\% - 30\% = 70\%$
$\frac{70}{100} \times 40 = 28$ gal.

25.

26. **$72**
$\$1,440 \div 20 = \$72$

27. **$\frac{13}{25}$**
$52\% = \frac{52}{100} = \frac{13}{25}$

28. **6 years 5 months**
19 years 3 months = $(19 \times 12) + 3$
$= 231$ months
$231 \div 3 = 77$ months
77 months = 6 years 5 months

29. **$13,562.50**
Interest = $\$12,500 \times 8.5\% \times 1$
$= \$1,062.50$
$\$12,500 + \$1,062.50 = \$13,562.50$

30. **65°**
$\angle ABC = 180° - 65° - 27°$
$= 88°$ (sum of $\angle$s in a triangle = 180°)
$\angle ABC = 180° - 27°$
$= 153°$ ($\angle$s between parallel sides add up to 180°)
$153° - 88° = 65°$

31. **40%**
$6,055 - 3,633 = 2,422$
$\frac{2,422}{6,055} \times 100 = 40\%$

32. **$468**
$\$1.95 \times 20 \times 12 = \$468$

33. **46,656 cm³**
$36 \times 36 \times 36 = 46,656$

Singapore Math Practice Level 5B

34. **208.05**
   Press C 3 1 2 0 . 7 5 ÷ 1 5 =

35. **416.65**
   Press C 3 2 . 0 5 × 1 3 =

36. $900 - 720 = 180$
   $0.75 = \frac{75}{100} = 75\%$
   $100\% - 75\% = 25\%$
   $\frac{25}{100} \times 180 = 45$
   45 students take Latin.

37. ∠FGJ $= 180° - 68° - 48°$
         $= 64°$ (sum of ∠s in a triangle = 180°)
   ∠FGH $= 180° - 64°$
         $= 116°$ (∠s on a straight line)
   ∠EFG $= 180° - 116°$
         $= \textbf{64°}$ (∠s between parallel sides add up to 180°)

38. ∠SQR $= (180° - 134°) ÷ 2$
         $= 23°$ (isosceles triangle)
   ∠PQR = ∠PRQ = ∠RPQ $= 60°$ (equilateral triangle)
   ∠SQP $= 23° + 60° = \textbf{83°}$

39. $5 \times 790 = 3,950$
   $2,910 + 3,950 = 6,860$
   $6,860 ÷ 7 = 980$
   The average number of visitors per day in a week is **980**.

40. (a) $\$2,999 + \$699 = \$3,698$
        $\frac{7}{100} \times \$3,698 = \$258.86$
        She paid **$258.86** in tax.
   (b) $\$3,698 + \$258.86 = \$3,956.86$
        She paid **$3,956.86** altogether.

41. **(See Diagram 10 on page 127)**
   Step 1: Draw Line BC 7 cm long using a ruler.
   Step 2: Draw an angle of 44° at Point B using a protractor.
   Step 3: Extend the line drawn from Point B to 2 cm using the ruler. Label this line as BA.
   Step 4: Draw Line AD using the ruler and set square. Make sure AD is parallel to Line BC.
   Step 5: Draw an angle of 38° at Point C using a protractor. Join Points C and D by drawing a line using the ruler.

42. $20\% + 32\% = 52\%$
   $52\% \rightarrow \$585$
   $1\% \rightarrow \$585 ÷ 52 = \$11.25$
   $100\% \rightarrow 100 \times \$11.25 = \$1,125$
   Eli's salary is **$1,125**.

43. $0.45 = \frac{45}{100}$
   $\frac{45}{100} \times 60 \text{ kg} = 27 \text{ kg}$
   $\frac{33}{100} \times 60 \text{ kg} = 19.8 \text{ kg}$
   $60 - 27 - 19.8 = 13.2 \text{ kg}$
   $13.2 \times 1,000 = 13,200 \text{ g}$
   $13,200 ÷ 120 = 110$
   He packed **110** 120-g bags of flour.

44. $1.5 \times \$12.40 = \$18.60$
   $(\$12.40 \times 8) + (\$18.60 \times 2) = \$136.40$
   $5 \times \$136.40 = \$682$
   Henry earns **$682**.

45. $31 - 17 = 14 \text{ in.}$
   $35 \times 19 \times 14 = 9,310 \text{ in.}^3$
   The volume of water needed to fill the tank completely is **9,310 in.³**.

46. 9 hr. 36 min. $= (9 \times 60) + 36$
                 $= 576 \text{ min.}$
   $576 ÷ 12 = 48$
   $48 \times 4 = 192$
   She could have drawn **192** patterns in 9 hours and 36 minutes.

47. 1.5 hr. $= 1.5 \times 60 = 90 \text{ min.}$
   $90 ÷ 5 = 18$
   $18 \times 200 = 3,600$
   The machine can pack **3,600** bars of soap in 1.5 hours.

48. (a) $1\frac{1}{2}$ hr. = 90 min.
        $1.6 \times 90 = 144 \text{ L}$
        $144 \times 1,000 = 144,000 \text{ mL}$
                     $= 144,000 \text{ cm}^3$
        144,000 cm³ of water will be in the tank after $1\frac{1}{2}$ hours.
   (b) $80 \times 60 \times 120 = 576,000 \text{ cm}^3$
        $1.6 \text{ L} = 1,600 \text{ cm}^3$
        $576,000 ÷ 1,600 = 360 \text{ min}$
        $360 ÷ 60 = 6 \text{ h}$
        It will take **6 hours** for the tank to be completely filled.

Challenge Questions

1. $4 \times 4.4 = 17.6$
   Let the smallest number be A.
   $A + (A + 1.1) + (A + 2.2) + (A + 3.3) = 17.6$
                                 $4A = 17.6 - 6.6$
                                   $A = 11 ÷ 4$
                                     $= 2.75$
   The smallest number is **2.75**.

2. Find the LCM of 2, 3, and 6.

        2 | 2, 3, 6
        3 | 1, 3, 3 $2 \times 3 = 6$
           | 1, 1, 1

   The LCM of 2, 3, and 6 is 6.
   The possible values of Y are:
      $6 + 1 = 7$
   $12 + 1 = 13$
   $18 + 1 = 19$
   The possible values of Y are **7**, **13**, and **19**.

3. Analyze the possibilities of all digits.
   First digit : 9
   Second digit : 2, 4, 6, or 8
   Third digit : 1, 3, 5, or 7

Singapore Math Practice Level 5B

Last digit : 60% of 1 = 0.6 (not possible)
60% of 3 = 1.8 (not possible)
60% of 5 = 3
60% of 7 = 4.2 (not possible)
The 4-digit number should be 9̲ 4 5̲ 3̲.
Check if the sum is 21.
$$9 + 4 + 5 + 3 = 21$$
I am **9,453**.

4. Find the LCM of 3 and 6.

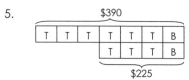

$$3 \times 2 = 6$$

Multiples of 6 between 70 and 100 = 72, 78, 84, 90, and 96
Possible values of X = 73, 79, 85, 91, and 97
The greatest possible value of X is **97**.

5.

$390

T	T	T	T	T	T	B
			T	T	T	B

$225

$390 − $225 = $165
$165 ÷ 3 = $55
A tennis racket cost $55.
$225 − (3 × $55) = $60
A basketball cost $60.
$60 + $55 = $115
The tennis racket and the basketball cost **$115**.

6. Analyze the possibilities of the third and fourth digits.
Third digit: 4, 5, 6
Fourth digit: 7, 8, 9
Use the Guess and Check method,
$(8 + 3 + \boxed{4} + \boxed{7} + 6 + 5) \div 5 = 6 \text{ R } 3$
$(8 + 3 + \boxed{5} + \boxed{8} + 6 + 5) \div 5 = 7$
$(8 + 3 + \boxed{6} + \boxed{9} + 6 + 5) \div 5 = 7 \text{ R } 2$
$(8 + 3 + \boxed{4} + \boxed{7} + 6 + 5) \div 6 = 5 \text{ R } 3$

The code is **8 3 4̲ 7̲ 6 5**.

7. Find the LCM of 6, 8, and 12.

```
3 | 6, 8, 12
2 | 2, 8, 4
2 | 1, 4, 2        3 × 2 × 2 × 2 = 24
2 | 1, 2, 1
  | 1, 1, 1
```

Multiple of 24 between 40 and 60 is 48.
48 ÷ 6 = 8, 48 ÷ 8 = 6, 48 ÷ 12 = 4
Sunita bought **48** stickers.

8. Analyze the possibilities of the first and last digits.
The last digit must be 0.
The first digit can only be 6 or 8.
In order to adhere to rules (a) to (d) and (f), the possible 7-digit numbers are: 8,326,490, 8,329,460, 8,346,290, and 8,349,260
Test each of the possible 7-digit numbers to see if it adheres to rule (e). Only 8,326,490 adheres to rule (e).
The 7-digit number is **8,326,490**.

9. $Z \div 5 = \text{quotient}$
quotient + 3 = 24
quotient − 3 = 18
∴ quotient = 24 − 3 = 18 + 3 = 21
$Z \div 5 = 21$
$Z = 21 \times 5 = 105$
Number Z is **105**.

10. By working backward, the percentage of ora‗e juice
Elena's children drank $= \frac{11}{10} \times 30\% = 33\% + 3($
$= 63\%$
Percentage of orange juice left = 100% − 3(·63%
= 7%
7% → 315 mL
1% → 315 ÷ 7 = 45 mL
100% → 45 × 100 = 4,500 mL
Aunt Elena made **4,500 mL** of orange juic‗

11. First number = A
Second number $= \frac{2}{5}A + 1A$
$= 1\frac{2}{5}A$
Third number $= \left(\frac{2}{5} \times 1\frac{2}{5}A\right) + 1\frac{2}{5}A$
$= \frac{14}{25}A + 1\frac{2}{5}A$
$= 1\frac{24}{25}A$
$A + 1\frac{2}{5}A + 1\frac{24}{25}A = 36\frac{1}{3} \times 3 = 109$
$4\frac{9}{25}A = 109$
$A = 109 \div 4\frac{9}{25}$
$A = 109 \div \frac{109}{25}$
$A = \cancel{109} \times \frac{25}{\cancel{109}}$
$A = 25$
$1\frac{24}{25} \times 25 = \frac{49}{\cancel{25}} \times \cancel{25} = 49$
The largest number is **49**.

12.

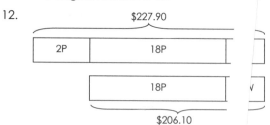

$227.90

$206.10

P: pizza   CW: chicken wings
2P = $227.90 − $206.10 = $21.80
P = $21.80 ÷ 2 = $10.90
CW = $206.10 − (18 × $10.90)
= $9.90
(4 × $10.90) + (4 × $9.90) = $83.20
4 pizzas and 4 boxes of chicken ‗‗gs cost **$83.20**.

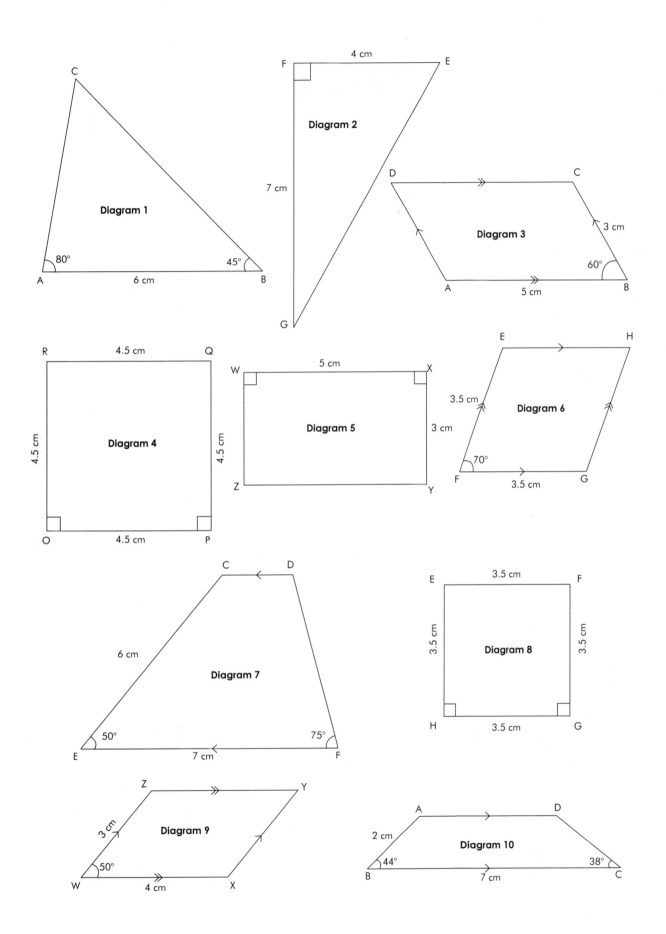

Diagram 1

C, A 80°, B 45°, 6 cm

Diagram 2

F, 4 cm, E, 7 cm, D, C, G

Diagram 3

D, C, 3 cm, 60°, A, 5 cm, B

Diagram 4

R, 4.5 cm, Q, 4.5 cm, 4.5 cm, O, 4.5 cm, P

Diagram 5

W, 5 cm, X, 3 cm, Z, Y

Diagram 6

E, H, 3.5 cm, 70°, F, 3.5 cm, G

Diagram 7

C, D, 6 cm, 50°, E, 7 cm, 75°, F

Diagram 8

E, 3.5 cm, F, 3.5 cm, 3.5 cm, H, 3.5 cm, G

Diagram 9

Z, Y, 3 cm, 50°, W, 4 cm, X

Diagram 10

A, D, 2 cm, 44°, B, 7 cm, 38°, C

Notes